This book is dedicated to my sister Kate, as we share a common enthusiasm for herbs, presents, families and special occasions.

CONTENTS

HERBAL GIFTS

Easy–to–make ideas that
capture the flavours, scents
and qualities of herbs

JOANNA SHEEN

CASSELL

Acknowledgements

My thanks to all at Ward Lock for their help on this project and to Jane Struthers for her editing skills.

I would especially like to thank Mandy Holmes of Busy Bee Crafts for all her help with the sewing projects in this book, Kate Baigent for help with the cookery for the photography and Diana Hatherly for inspiration all the way through!

A CASSELL BOOK

First published in hardback
in the UK 1991
by Ward Lock
(a Cassell imprint)
Villiers House
41/47 Strand
LONDON
WC2N 5JE

First published in paperback 1992
Reprinted 1993

British Library Cataloguing in Publication Data
Sheen, Joanna
  Herbal gifts.
  1 Herbs
  I. Title
  641.357

  ISBN 0-304-34272-6 (paperback)

Typeset by Columns Design and Production Services Ltd, Reading

Printed and bound in Singapore by Kyodo Printing Ltd

INTRODUCTION

If you are looking for inspiration for an unusual present you can often turn to the pages of a history book for inspiring ideas. Beautiful little posies of flowers, or tussie-mussies, as they were called in the sixteenth century, make a lovely gift for a hostess and can convey a particular message, using the language and symbolism of flowers. They were originally made to mask the smells and give protection from the germs of those days of plague and poor sewerage, but gradually they became carriers of secret messages between friends and lovers, using the language of flowers. If you want to continue this tradition, a wide selection of the meanings of flowers is given as an appendix at the end of this book. Herbal posies are simple to make but look wonderful and give a great deal of pleasure.

A selection of herbal teas could be a good way to introduce someone to the subtleties of herbal tisanes and mixtures. There are many herbal mixtures that give gentle relief from everyday stresses and strains and can help with minor problems. Herbs and wild fruits can be collected and made into lovely kitchen produce, and all cooks would love to receive some of the goodies featured in the kitchen section.

Herbal concoctions for use in the bathroom are a real luxury. Your own herbal cosmetics and beauty treatments will probably be asked for again and again, and it's easy to become addicted to mixing your own potions and lotions. There are many ideas in the Beautiful Herbs chapter, most of which you will want to keep once you have made them, so perhaps you should always make double the quantity!

Although it seems easier to buy attractive presents for friends, they would much rather receive something that you had spent your time and patience making especially for them. This book will inspire you and gives clear instructions on how to make the suggested projects and present them in a really attractive way.

You will find many ideas, both old and new, that will inspire you to use and grow herbs and to make the most of your herbal crop. There are plenty of different projects to turn a herbal harvest into delightful presents for a wide variety of people — perhaps even yourself! Giving is a habit to be encouraged as there are few things more enjoyable than giving a special present that pleases a friend. Finding time to create things yourself can be wonderfully calming as you become absorbed in the task and enjoy the reactions of your family and friends when they receive your special offerings!

HERBS IN THE GARDEN

Herbs have been grown and harvested for many centuries, during which time man has experimented with their medicinal and culinary uses very successfully. For example, there are many remedies mentioned in Culpeper's Herbal from the 1600s that are still popular today. Herbs should also be appreciated for their own beauty as plants and cut flowers, both in the garden and in the house. Many have very attractive flowers, and the soft foliage of southernwood or sage makes a lovely background for summer flowers. Most herbs are fairly simple to grow and do not demand much attention or special conditions.

THE HISTORY OF HERBS

The history of the use of herbs goes back a long time, because they were undoubtedly being eaten and used semi-medicinally long before anyone knew how to write down their uses. The Bible mentions herbs and spices in the Old Testament in the book of Exodus when Moses leads the Israelites across the desert, and in Genesis, the word 'herb' is used to describe plants in general. Most civilizations have used herbs medicinally — the ancient Greeks had several famous healers with a wide knowledge of herbs and their medicinal uses. Asclepius lived in 1300 BC and was so successful that he was eventually deified! Hippocrates, the father of medicine today, lived in 400 BC and his knowledge was recorded in his medical writings and formed some of the basis for modern scientific medicine.

Herbs and the Romans
The Romans made good use of herbs and carried them as portable first aid kits. Garlic was handed out to the troops to treat wounds and act as a general strengthening medicament, and the juice was used as a natural disinfectant. Even today, garlic is used as a mild antibiotic and can be taken as a protection against the common cold. When the Romans invaded Britain they brought their herbs

Herbs make an attractive and colourful addition to any garden as well as being invaluable for culinary, craft and beauty purposes.

with them and so naturalized many plants, such as rosemary, sage and thyme, that had previously grown around the Mediterranean. Once the British had been converted to Christianity, a network of monasteries developed throughout the land. As well as their religious duties, the monks acted as doctors, because they were knowledgeable about herbs and potions and had the time and ability to make a record of their uses. Illustrated texts and manuscripts on herbs were lovingly written by the monks and this information became far more widely available with the invention of printing.

The Middle Ages
The heyday of herbs came during the sixteenth and seventeenth centuries, when herbs were widely planted in both smaller domestic gardens and in the grounds of manor houses for use in still rooms. There were two particularly well-known herbalists of the time, John Gerard and Nicholas Culpeper. Although they are both equally famous for their works, Culpeper disagreed with much that Gerard had written and, in fact, disagreed with most that all the other herbalists had written too. Instead, he claimed links between astrology and herbs, starting a debate which still continues today.

The wife with a larger house to run, such as one of the manor houses of the time, would have had her own still room, where herbal medicaments, pot-pourri and other fragrant necessities were made. Recipes for potions to heal, perfume and disinfect the home were handed down through families. Herbs were still grown in monastery gardens but also in stylized gardens in the manor grounds. Small, well

clipped hedges of such herbs as cotton lavender, marjoram or thyme were usually grown, either on their own or with box as well.

Herbs were used for several purposes: to strew on floors to counteract the filth and vermin so prevalent in those days, to perfume the family members and help with beauty preparations and, last but not least, in cookery. Strong herbs were often essential to mask the taste of meat that was long past its prime, and so played a major role in the kitchen.

Setting sail for America
When the settlers began to populate America, they took herb plants and seeds with them as treasured possessions. There were very few doctors available, and those that were there may well have been deported for good reason anyway, so the settlers had to rely on their own herbal knowledge and remedies. The use of herbs continued strongly in America for the next hundred years or so, mainly promoted by the Shakers, a religious sect who developed a strong agricultural industry, growing and selling medicinal herbs.

The influence of Gertrude Jekyll
The popularity of herbs seemed to wane in Britain during the nineteenth century, possibly because of the Industrial Revolution and lack of respect for things old and tried. Trends shifted back towards herbs in the garden at the end of the century when Gertrude Jekyll, who worked first with William Robinson and later with Edwin Lutyens, made an unforgettable contribution to gardening landscaping and design. She had a very broad knowledge of plants and wrote many books which are still

popular today. Favourite plants of hers tended towards the soft greys and blues of the herb bed, mixing with the more vibrant cottage garden plants.

Herbs today
Lack of ingredients and a search for flavourings to brighten the rather uninspired range of foods available during the two World Wars led to a re-emergence of interest in herbs and herbal gardening in Britain during the early part of this century. Mrs Maude Grieve published *A Modern Herbal* in 1931 — this gave details of over a thousand herbs, their cultivation and habitats, and encouraged a new generation to explore unfamiliar herbal territories.

Country folk have always respected herbal lore and today the interest in all things herbal is gathering pace. Many modern herbalists are using the same herbs recommended by Culpeper — although we now know that vitamin C cures scurvy, Culpeper used scurvy-grass (*Cochlearia officinalis*) which has now been proved to contain vitamin C and is still recommended by some modern herbalists. There are many such examples in Culpeper's work and also some lively comments that give you an inkling of what a character he must have been.

Today, 'alternative' ideas have many followers and, although herbal medicine is not really part of this book, it is nevertheless a very interesting subject and worth investigating if you have a general interest in herbs. Many gift ideas have their roots in herbal history, and in this chapter you will find a few to set you thinking. All our cosmetics today are derived from the ladies' pills and potions concocted in still

Herbs have been grown for many centuries, by gardeners from all walks of life. They play an important role in our medical and culinary history.

rooms over the centuries, and herbal teas, although pleasant to drink, may in many cases have a medical background. There are several historical and literary sources that could inspire you to create presents that are unusual but very successful, so keep an open mind and don't be afraid to experiment.

GROWING YOUR OWN HERBS

Herbs can lend themselves to a very formal planting scheme in the style of an Elizabethan knot garden or a stylized maze or cartwheel design. Alternatively, you can treat herbs as traditional cottage garden plants and aim for the less formal, country style. Lovely soft plants like *Alchemilla mollis* can drape over the edge of winding paths, and large, old-fashioned bushes of lavender can form their own focal point in a natural garden.

The range of colours in herbal plant varieties is wide, but the greys, silvery blues and hazy lilacs seem to predominate. A colour scheme can be planned alongside the overall planting scheme or it can develop as the garden does, gently over several years. Many of the prettiest country gardens are the product of many years' work — perhaps not intensive planning so much as general loving care and attention to plants, and an eager eye that collects new plants whenever the opportunity arises. Many herbs grow well from cuttings or inexpensively from seed, so gathering a collection of herb plants need not be time-consuming or expensive.

There is a multitude of possible herbs that you could choose to grow, and similarly a multitude of books on herb gardening that offer advice and expertise on the care of your plants. In this book, my main aim is to give ideas and inspiration for products that can be made from your herbal harvest. Assuming that you have few herbs growing in your garden already (although you may be surprised at how many you do have!), I am going to recommend a basic list of twenty herbs that really are well worth growing.

TOP TWENTY HERBS

This is a purely personal selection of the twenty herbs I use most often. They can be used to make teas, in cookery, pot-pourris and for decorative drying purposes.

1. Lady's mantle (*Alchemilla mollis*)
This is a beautiful plant which looks lovely growing in the garden. It is a hardy perennial and can be propagated by division in the spring or autumn. The flowers dry well with the air-drying method and also glycerine beautifully. They are very useful additions to fresh or dried flower bouquets and posies. The flowers press well in small sprays for pressed flower work. The leaves can be infused and applied as a skin tonic once the concoction has been chilled in the fridge. The whole plant can be infused and drunk as a medicinal tea to help relieve the symptoms of diarrhoea and also to relieve menopausal problems.

2. Wormwood (*Artemisia absinthium* 'Lambrook Silver') **or Southernwood** (*Artemisia abrotanum*)
Both of these are hardy plants that are very easy to grow and can be propagated from cuttings in the early autumn. The fine silvery foliage looks most attractive in the garden and is also very useful in fresh flower posies or for pressed flower or dried flower arrangements.

When dried, the leaves are useful in pot-pourris and also are important ingredients in anti-moth sachets for wardrobes.

3. Rue — especially 'Jackman's Blue' (*Ruta graveolens*)

This is a hardy evergreen shrub which you can propagate by division in the spring or from cuttings in the early autumn. The seed heads can be dried for decorative use and the leaves can be pressed or glycerined. An attractive plant for the garden, rue is also useful for fresh tussie-mussies. Rue is often an ingredient in anti-moth sachets and small amounts can be used in cooking.

4. Cotton lavender — particularly 'Lemon Queen' (*Santolina chamaecyparissus*)

Here is another hardy evergreen shrub that gives some silver colour to the borders. It can be propagated from cuttings throughout most of the summer and early autumn. 'Lemon Queen' has a particularly pretty cream-coloured flower rather than the normal bright yellow of the other varieties. Another variety that I would recommend is *Santolina neapolitana*, because the foliage is very attractive. In addition to its fresh, dried and pressed decorative uses, this herb is good in anti-moth sachets and for general use in pot-pourris — it gives a pretty silvery lift to your mixture.

5. Feverfew (*Chrysanthemum parthenium*)

A hardy perennial, this little plant self-seeds profusely, but if you prefer, cuttings and division seem to work well. The variety that I would recommend is 'Aureum', the golden feverfew, which has bright lime green leaves and gives a cheerful splash of colour to any planting scheme. When dried, the flowers are useful in pot-pourris. The leaves can be eaten or infused as a tea, and are said to help migraine sufferers.

6. Hop (*Humulus lupulus*)

A hardy but deciduous climber, the hop really is a very striking and beautiful plant to grow, because it can trail over a pergola, up a fence or even over a special frame. The dried flowers and leaves look lovely in arrangements or in swags and garlands and, of course, the female flowers are used to make beer. Hop pillows are considered to be sleep-inducing, and an infusion of flowers with a little honey can be calming and also helps with hangovers!

7. Heather (*Calluna vulgaris*)

This hardy shrub can be most useful in the garden as it needs very little maintenance and looks extremely pretty, especially when in flower. Heather can be dried but the results are much better when the sprigs of flowers are preserved in glycerine. Obviously very useful in fresh or dried decorative work, the sprigs also look attractive in pot-pourris. For medicinal purposes, young heather tips can be infused as a tea and are also apparently very helpful for such skin problems as freckles and spots, and as a general aid to the complexion.

8. Clove pink (*Dianthus caryophyllus*)

Although a perennial, this plant can be rather short-lived, especially if there are fierce frosts. Propagation is very easy, from stem cuttings taken in the spring, so constant stocks can be maintained. 'Doris' is a very well-known variety and has a lovely perfume, but there are many different types from which to choose. The flowers can be preserved in silica gel to use as decorations for pot-pourris or air-dried for inclusion in arrangements. The flowers are also useful when making floral vinegars, jams and wines and can be infused in wine as a nerve tonic.

Growing herbs for use in pot pourri or to add fragrance to flower arrangements is another facet of a herb garden that should not be forgotten.

9. Lavender (*Lavandula angustifolia*)
A hardy evergreen shrub, lavender is highly recommended in the garden as it looks pretty all year round, but obviously it is at its best during the flowering season in the summer. Stem cuttings are easily propagated in either spring or autumn and there are many varieties of lavender from which to choose. 'Hidcote' is a very popular dark purple variety and 'Alba', a white form, makes a good contrast. There are also other species, such as *Lavandula stoechas*, or French lavender, that have very interesting shapes. Lavender has a great many uses, some of which are quite unusual and not well-known. It can be very useful in the kitchen for making lavender vinegars, oils and mustards. Of course, it has always been one of the chief ingredients of pot-pourri, and lavender sachets are lovely tucked into linen and clothes. The essential oil is an excellent antidote to insect bites, stings and burns, and when a few drops are added to the bathwater, the effect is very relaxing. (It is especially good for grumpy children!)

10. Borage (*Borago officinalis*)
Borage is a hardy annual and although it self-seeds fairly freely it may be necessary to grow new plants each year. The flowers press beautifully but the plant does not really lend itself to drying. The flowers can be crystallized for cake decorating and the leaves are excellent in Pimms No. 1. They can also be mixed with soft cheeses or used to decorate all sorts of foods.

11. Mint (*Mentha* sp.)
There are many mints in this family, all of which are hardy perennials. They can be propagated by root division or from cuttings, but as they are mostly very invasive I would suggest they are planted in pots or bags sunk into the earth, as that will contain their roots. The most popular use for mint is in the kitchen — mint sauce or jelly are the essential accompaniments to roast lamb and mint leaves are delicious flavouring for new potatoes and peas. The best types of mint for these purposes are spearmint, applemint or the upright pennyroyal. Mint is very useful as a tea to help relieve colds and hiccups. The tea can also be used as an effective hair rinse and, because the dried herb has a relaxing effect, it can be added to sleep pillows. The common spearmint and peppermint both work well for this. For fragrant uses and herbal posies, the variegated applemint looks superb and the eau-de-Cologne mint smells wonderful.

12. Rosemary (*Rosmarinus officinalis*)
This hardy evergreen perennial likes a sunny position and can be propagated from cuttings. Rosemary is best known for its culinary use with lamb and pork, but it also mixes well with vegetables. It is very useful in pot-pourri, and it glycerines beautifully, turning a greyish colour. The leaves infused as a tea help the digestion and a strong infusion of the tea has a very invigorating effect when mixed into the bathwater. The oil of rosemary can also be diluted and used as a final rinse when washing the hair.

13. Alecost or Costmary (*Chrysanthemum balsamita*)
This hardy perennial prefers full sun and can be divided in the spring or autumn. Originally used in beer (hence the name 'alecost'), it is now more popularly used to flavour vegetables, poultry or game. When dried, the leaves are very useful for pot-pourri mixes as they help strengthen other scents in the mix. The herb is also an insect repellent and can be made up into a fragrant washing water and used to scent linen.

14. Thyme (*Thymus* sp.)

The thyme family are all evergreen shrubs and can be propagated from cuttings or seed. In fresh posies they add a distinctive aroma, but are best known for their culinary uses. Thyme makes a soothing tea for those with chest complaints or sleeping problems. The dried leaves can be added to pot-pourris and, when used as a facial steam, they clear the complexion. Many recipes call for thyme, particularly stocks, marinades and stuffings.

15. Rose (*Rosa* sp.)

Roses are hardy shrubs that can either be bought as plants or propagated from cuttings in the autumn. The fragrant old-fashioned roses are a wonderful addition to any garden, and a variety such as *Rosa rubrigosa* has very pretty hips. The flowers look stunning in fresh and dried arrangements but roses have many other uses too. The petals can be used fresh in salads or crystallized for decorations. Rose sorbet is very unusual and has a delicate taste. The hips can be used in teas, wines, cordials and jams. Rosewater is a tonic that is particularly suited to dry or mature skins. The dry petals are also a major component in pot-pourris.

16. Lemon verbena (*Aloysia triphylla*)

A half-hardy shrub, lemon verbena needs the protection of a greenhouse during the winter otherwise frosts can kill it. Cuttings can be taken in the spring. The dried leaves are a very useful addition to pot-pourri and other perfumed ideas, including an infusion to fill finger bowls. Pads soaked in the infusion and placed on the eyes reduce puffiness, and the tea eases bronchial and nasal congestion. When mixed with apples, it makes a lovely fragrant jelly.

17. Fennel (*Foeniculum vulgare*)

Fennel is a hardy herbaceous perennial that can be divided in the autumn. However, it self-seeds so efficiently that it is usually a case of weeding extra plants out rather than putting them in! It is important not to plant fennel too near dill, as cross-pollination can occur and then the subtle flavours are lost. The flowers can be air-dried or preserved in glycerine. The bronze form is especially pretty in the garden and can be chewed to sweeten the breath. Both the seeds and leaves can be used as a facial steam to deep cleanse the skin, and an infusion of tea aids digestion. Chop the leaves over vegetables and fish.

18. Basil (*Ocimum basilicum*)

Basil is a tender annual and does not rate as the easiest herb to grow, but it is well worth the effort entailed. The plants are very prone to 'damping off', and overwatering must be avoided. It may be worth growing basil in a pot indoors or in a greenhouse. The purple variety looks very effective in the garden and also as part of a dried herb wreath or decoration. When infused as a tea it has mild antiseptic qualities and can relieve nausea. Basil is very well-known for its culinary uses and goes very well with tomatoes and garlic dishes. An infusion of the leaves in bathwater makes a fresh and invigorating bath.

19. Camomile (*Chamaemelum nobile*)

A hardy evergreen perennial, camomile can be propagated from cuttings or by division. The variety 'Flore-pleno' is double flowered and dries well for use in decorations. Both the flowers and leaves are good in pot-pourris. An infusion used regularly lightens the hair and a camomile tea is a good tonic. The tea is especially recommended for restless children and for preventing nightmares, so maybe that explains why Peter Rabbit was given a dose of it in the Beatrix Potter story! Camomile tea bags placed on the eyes reduce puffiness and help to lighten shadows under the eyes.

*There is a wide variety of herbs that
are useful in the kitchen, but a selection
of sages, rosemary and various mints
are definitely the most popular.*

20. Scented geraniums (*Pelargonium* sp.)
These scented geraniums are all tender evergreen perennials and must be moved indoors or into a greenhouse for the winter. Cuttings root well in sand and are easy to take. There are many different varieties and scents from which to choose, including lemon, orange, rose and peppermint. It is well worth building a small collection of these plants, especially for pot-pourris. They have several culinary uses too, particularly in sorbets, jellies and syrups. When the leaves are infused they make a good mild astringent and when put into bath bags they give a wonderfully aromatic bath.

SPECIAL HERB COLLECTIONS

If space is at a premium, or you have a tidy mind, you might like to grow your herbs in groups according to their uses. A garden filled predominantly with herbs always looks lovely, but small collections for a specific purpose are interesting and create a good talking point. I have devised several collections, each comprising of ten plants, but you could alter my choices to suit your own requirements.

Culinary herbs

A culinary collection is most convenient if it is sited near the kitchen, by the back door or even on the windowsill inside or outside the window. It may sound lazy to suggest that it takes too long to wander down the garden to find the necessary herbs for the meal you are cooking, but on days when the weather is bad you will be far more inclined to reach just outside the back door for a piece of foliage than to get wet walking through the garden!

My choice for the ten culinary herbs to grow is as follows, but is not necessarily in order of preference!

1. Borage (*Borago officinalis*)
The leaves add the flavour of cucumber to cold drinks and the flowers are very useful for crystallizing.

2. Chives (*Allium schoenoprasum*)
The flowers can be used in salads and the leaves are chopped as a garnish for soups, salads and vegetables. Chives are lovely with cream cheese.

3. Dill (*Anethum graveolens*)
The leaves are delicious in pickles — particularly with gherkins — and are also good with salmon and new potatoes. They also go well with eggs and potato salads.

4. Basil (*Ocium basilicum*)
Basil is marvellous with tomato and garlic dishes for that real Mediterranean flavour!

5. Mint (*Mentha* sp.)
These herbs are invaluable for vinegars, sauces, syrups and jellies. Young leaves are delicious when added to new potatoes, peas and fruit salads and summer drinks.

6. Parsley (*Petroselinum crispum*)
This is a very popular culinary herb which can be used as a garnish in large sprigs or chopped finely and sprinkled over a wide variety of dishes. If added to a dish while it is cooking, parsley should not be incorporated in the early stages.

7. Thyme (*Thymus* sp.)
Another very popular kitchen herb often used in stuffing poultry, thyme is also very useful with vegetables and in jellies.

8. Sage (*Salvia officinalis*)
Sage is very useful with the fattier meats such

as duck or pork. It is particularly good with liver and sausages. Sage and apple jelly is delicious.

9. Marjoram/oregano (*Origanum* sp.)
Marjoram is delicious with fish and in cream or butter sauces, and oregano is used with pizzas, tomatoes and egg dishes.

10. Chervil (*Anthriscus cerefolium*)
Chervil is delicious with vegetables, particularly carrots, and with white fish and chicken. It should always be added towards the end of the cooking time.

Aromatic herbs
The aromatic qualities of dried flowers and leaves are very important. Pot-pourri has been used in the home for many centuries to scent a room gently or deodorize unpleasant smells, and the natural antiseptic qualities of some herbs can protect against unwanted insects, whether they be moths, fleas or worse!

These plants look lovely as a collection of fresh flowers or leaves in a posy. You could also plant them around a seating area in the garden so you can enjoy their scents while you relax.

1. Lemon verbena (*Aloysia triphylla*)
Once dried, the leaves give a delicious scent to pot-pourris and can also be used to scent ink and writing paper. The essential oil is often used in perfumes. The leaves smell delicious when rubbed.

2. Clove pink (*Dianthus caryophyllus*)
These flowers look very decorative in the garden and have a lovely distinctive perfume. They can be dried and used in pot-pourris.

3. Lavender (*Lavandula angustifolia*)
This is a very necessary ingredient of pot-pourris as it features in many recipes. It has a number of other aromatic uses around the house, particularly when made into sachets and bunches.

4. Bergamot (*Monarda didyma*)
Both the flowers and the leaves can be used when dry in pot-pourris. The scarlet flowers retain their colour well.

5. Myrtle (*Myrtus communis*)
The creamy flowers and dark green leaves look pretty in pot-pourris and the leaves are particularly aromatic.

6. Scented geranium (*Pelargonium* sp.)
The leaves are very strongly fragranced and make a delightful addition to sachets, pillows and open pot-pourris. There are various scented pelargoniums to choose from and all are equally useful, so it is just a matter of personal taste as to which ones you grow.

7. Sweet violet (*Viola odorata*)
This is a lovely flower to use in floral waters and perfumes. Dry both the flowers and the leaves to add to pot-pourris.

8. Rose (*Rosa* sp.)
These flowers are a vital ingredient of this collection — particularly the old-fashioned scented varieties. Both the petals and hips are useful for pot-pourris. Rose petals have been the basis for all types of pot-pourri through the ages.

9. French marigold (*Tagetes patula*)
The leaves of the different varieties have different scents, some orange, some lemon. Both the scented leaves and the coloured flowers are good for pot-pourris.

10. Angelica (*Angelica archangelica*)
This is a pretty plant for the garden. Angelica seed gives off a lovely smell when burnt and the leaves and roots are useful for pot-pourris.

Herbal teas

Herbal teas made from freshly picked ingredients from the garden are incomparably better than those made from dried leaf or flower infusions. Although it is not practical to grow a vast number of plants for tea-making, I have chosen a small selection that cover fairly everyday problems and are moderately easy to grow.

These teas are meant to be taken as enjoyable drinks or as mild remedies for very minor problems. If in doubt, see your doctor and don't attempt to treat yourself.

1. Camomile (*Chamaemelum nobile*)
The flowers are dried to make teas and are regarded by some as a panacea for all ills! Camomile aids restful sleep and is excellent for soothing indigestion and nerves.

2. Comfrey (*Symphytum officinale*)
Tea can be made from fresh or dried material and drunk to alleviate the pain caused by piles. It is also a very effective cure for diarrhoea.

3. Heather (*Calluna vulgaris*)
Tea can be made from the fresh flowering tips to help clear the complexion, to remove freckles and to help acne.

4. Fennel (*Foeniculum vulgare*)
Fennel leaves and seeds can be infused and the tea drunk as a stimulant. According to an old wives' tale, fennel tea is meant to help with a slimming regime and as a general relaxant.

There are many traditional recipes for herbal teas that have marvellous healing properties. Growing the herbs so that they can be gathered fresh from your own garden makes a world of difference to the taste of your brew!

5. Hop (*Humulus lupulus*)
The flowers make a tea that calms the nerves and also acts as a tonic and stimulates the appetite. Add honey or sugar for flavour.

6. Lovage (*Ligusticum scoticum*)
Although lovage has a rather strong flavour it is very useful as a gargle and helps to soothe sore throats. It also helps to dispel flatulence.

7. Sweet cicely (*Myrrhis odorata*)
Sweet cicely tea is a relaxing and refreshing drink which can help to soothe persistent coughs and ease sore throats.

8. Caraway (*Carum carvi*)
Caraway tea can be made from the leaves and stalks of young caraway plants to give a gentle relaxing tea. Tea made from the crushed seeds is much stronger in flavour but a better relaxant.

9. Feverfew (*Chrysanthemum parthenium*)
This tea is currently very popular as a relief from migraine and headaches in general. The leaves should be infused to make the tea and in many cases it really does work.

10. Lungwort (*Pulmonaria officinalis*)
The tea made from lungwort leaves is useful for helping persistent coughs and lung disorders (hence the common name).

PRESERVING YOUR CROP

There are four possible ways to preserve plants and they are as follows:

Air-drying

Plants need to be picked in the early to mid-morning, when the dew has evaporated but before the sun gets too hot and draws out the oils. When picking them, never mix different varieties of herb, try to keep them well separated and tie them into small bunches which can then be hung up in a well-ventilated warm place with as little light as possible. You could use an airing cupboard or warm area near the boiler, if it is dark enough. Alternatively, a dark corner in a spare bedroom works well or, if it is warm and dry enough, a loft or attic could be used. The kitchen can sometimes be sufficiently warm, but take care not to hang the drying herbs near the steam of a kettle or moisture from the sink, otherwise they will just go mouldy. Once hung up, the leaves or flowers can take from four to five days to a couple of weeks to dry.

When they are completely dry, the herbs can be stored in layers in a box, each layer separated by tissue paper. Make sure that the box is kept in a warm dry place and that no mice or insects can make their way inside for a feast! Air-drying is suitable for the majority of herbs that are used for pot-pourri mixtures, herbal teas (although fresh herbs, when available, are usually preferable) and dried decorative arrangements.

Herbs can also be dried in a microwave oven on a low setting, but the time and temperature needed will vary according to the wattage of your microwave and the amount of material you are drying. Experiment by placing a small amount of herbs on a piece of kitchen paper in the microwave and put it on a fairly low setting for a couple of minutes. Take note of how well the herbs have dried and add or subtract seconds, and lower or raise the heat, with the next batch until you get the desired results.

Freezing

When herbs are intended for culinary use, freezing them can give a better flavour than drying them. The leaves should be removed from the main stalk, then washed and dried if necessary. They can then be packed into small polythene bags and clearly labelled. Never put into a bag more than you think you might use for one dish as the herbs will not keep well once defrosted. Another way to freeze herbs is to fill ice cube trays with their finely chopped leaves and top up with water. As a general rule, each ice cube contains one tablespoonful of chopped herbs.

Drying with silica gel crystals

This method is particularly useful if you want beautiful flowers for the top of pot-pourri mixtures or are using herbal flowers in decorative arrangements, because the flowers are preserved intact. The flower heads should be lightly wired before they are dried so the stems can be extended after drying if necessary. Push a lightweight wire through the centre of each flower and trim it so it is no more than about 2 in (5 cm) long at the most.

Silica gel is available from floral outlets, garden centres and chemists. The crystals must be as fine as possible and dry.

Using an old biscuit tin or plastic airtight container, fill the container to a depth of about 1 in (2.5 cm) with the crystals. Carefully place the flowers on to the bed of crystals and with a small spoon gently cover them with more crystals, filling in all the gaps and crevices as you go. When they are covered with the crystals, replace the lid and leave in a warm, dry place. The flower heads will usually be dry after about two or three days and can be carefully unpacked and stored in an airtight container with a little silica gel in the bottom to prevent any re-absorption of moisture.

Before you use it, you might like to spray the material that has been dried by this method with polyurethane varnish (matt), as this helps to prevent the moisture returning. However, this should not be a problem if the flowers are kept in a warm temperature.

Glycerine treatment

There are several herbs that respond well to this treatment, including *Alchemilla*, rosemary and fennel flowers. It is always worth experimenting to see which herbs respond to this treatment as a new result is always fascinating.

Mix glycerine and boiling water in a ratio of two parts water to one part glycerine (sometimes an equal amount of each is more successful) and fill a fairly narrow container to a depth of approximately 3–4 in (7.5–10 cm). Having smashed the stems if they are particularly woody, stand the material in the glycerine mixture out of direct light. It usually takes from between four days and two weeks for the plant material to take up the glycerine, but occasionally some may need longer.

Usually you can tell how far the glycerine has travelled because the plant visibly changes colour as it absorbs the mixture. If beads of glycerine are visible at the ends of the leaves you should remove them from the mixture straightaway and, if necessary, wipe away any excess glycerine with a soapy cloth before leaving them to dry.

The glycerined material should then be stored in a box away from light and moisture.

PRESSING HERBS

Flower pressing has been a popular craft since the Victorian days and many small treasures have been hidden away in family bibles and other such books. Today, telephone directories serve a similar, if more prosaic, purpose. Rather than pressing only the more usual garden flowers you could try making pictures and designs with herbs. The possibilities are endless: botanical-style pictures, decorated recipe cards, herbal gift tags and greetings cards with a packet of seeds for the recipient are just some of the ideas open to you. By referring to the language of flowers list in the back of the book you could make a design that also carries a subtle message for the person who will receive it.

PRESSING FLOWERS AND HERBS

Preserving flowers by pressing them is an age-old process that can be enjoyed by children and adults alike, and can be as complicated or straightforward as you wish. One of the simplest ways to press flowers and herbs is to place the small sprigs of herb or the individual flowers between sheets of blotting paper, insert them between the pages of a telephone directory and then put more weights on top.

Pressing material with a flower press
A slightly more sophisticated method involves using a standard flower press, which is usually available from craft shops or garden centres. This consists of two pieces of plywood with a hole in each of the corners. Threaded through each hole is a bolt with a wing nut on the end. I usually fill my press with ten layers of flowers, separated by sheets of newspaper and blotting paper, because any more layers than that become unmanageable.

Start with a layer of newspaper and then place a sheet of blotting paper on top of it. Lay out the flowers or herbs you wish to press on this, making sure that none overlap and they are all at least 1 in (2.5 cm) from the edge of the paper. Carefully cover them with more blotting paper and then place a layer of newspaper over that, followed by another sheet of blotting paper. Add more flowers and continue

These pressed flower pictures feature a selection of herbs, including borage, camomile, Artemisia, sage and rue. They are mixed with such cottage garden flowers as pansies, roses and love-in-a-mist.

until you have placed ten complete layers in the press. Finish with a layer of newspaper, then screw down the bolts. Label the press with a list of its contents and the date, and put it in a warm spot for approximately six to eight weeks, by which time the contents should be dry and ready to use. If you want to refill the press, the contents can be unpacked into cellophane-fronted paper bags. Thoroughly iron the used blotting paper and newspaper to remove any dampness, and then the process can start again.

Pressing herbs in the microwave
The majority of attractively shaped or coloured herbs are in shades of green, which is the first colour that fades from pressed material. However, pressing herbs in a microwave oven gives a better colour retention, so the colour will last longer than it normally does.

Take two pieces of 10 × 8 in (25 x 20 cm) hardboard and two pieces of blotting paper that are slightly smaller in size. Lay out a piece of hardboard, place a sheet of blotting paper on top and then arrange some pieces of herb on the blotting paper, making sure that none of them overlap or go over the edge. Cover them with the other sheet of blotting paper and then the second sheet of hardboard. Using five very strong elastic bands, hold the two pieces of board together by stretching three elastic bands along the 10 in (25 cm) length and two along the 8 in (20 cm) length. This should hold the 'sandwich' together very tightly.

Then place the package in the microwave on the lowest setting available to you (defrost or lower) and cook for approxi-

mately five minutes. The timing needed will vary according to the thickness of the material you are pressing, but five minutes is a fairly average time with which to start your experiments.

Leave the bundle to cool when it comes out of the oven and then check to see whether it is completely dry. If not, wrap it all up again with the elastic bands and cook for a further two to three minutes. Allow to cool and check again. When the material is completely dry and stiff, and has cooled down, it is ready for use.

The best way to master this technique is to try your own microwave and make notes on the drying times various materials have taken. Do take care to use a low setting only or the hardboard will catch fire — not a good start! A few herbs will not press, but the majority give very successful results.

MAKING A HERBAL PICTURE

In the picture on page 34, a collection of mainly culinary herbs has been arranged into an informal bouquet and displayed on a moss green mount. The centre flowers are *Clematis montana*, which have turned from a creamy tone to a pale beige and match the frame exactly. The herbs used in the picture include dill, lavender, thyme, sage, scented geraniums, lemon verbena, various mints and chervil.

The flowers are arranged on silk that is stretched across a mossy green coloured linen mount. The silk could be in any toning colour but cream is a gentle and neutral background that always seems to blend well with flowers and leaves. It can also look just as effective if you use a

cream card background. Once you have laid out the herbs and flowers you want to use, leave the picture for a while under a sheet of glass. When you return you may find you want to make a few alterations; it is far easier to make an objective criticism of your work if you have been away from it for a while.

When you are happy with it, the arrangement can be glued in place with a latex adhesive. If you have used a card backing, the design and mount can then be fitted into an ordinary photo frame with very little effort. If, however, you choose to do your design on a silk backing, the framing process is a little more complicated and the picture must have a piece of ½ in (12 mm) foam placed behind it or some wadding (as you would use in quilting) and a hardboard back fitted. The frame is then attached by tacking nails at right angles to the frame into the rebate to hold the sandwich of glass, mount, design, padding and hardboard back together. Alternatively, you can use a professional glazier's gun or ask your local picture framer to help you out!

Botanical themed pictures

Perhaps you could collect a little piece from all the herbs in your kitchen garden and make a design with an entirely culinary theme, or an aromatic collection of herbs in a picture. What a shame one can't smell through the glass!

Herbs also lend themselves very well to botanical-style pictures. You could collect and press all the different components of the plant, perhaps at differing months of the year, then display them in a simple way with a good quality frame. A lovely idea for a picture in a kitchen would be a

display of all the various types of mint, including applemint, pineapple mint and spearmint, all arranged and perhaps label-led in copperplate writing to give an antique feel to the design.

Other ideas for pictures

Shakespeare mentioned many herbs and wild flowers in his works, and a delightful picture could be made using all the flowers mentioned in a particular play or even a more general Shakespearian collage. Some of the better-known varieties named in Shakespearian plays are borage, clover, columbine, cowslip, daisies, larkspur, lavender, myrtle, roses, rosemary, rue, thyme, violet and winter savoury.

If you used roses, larkspur and daisies as your central flowers, a ruff of herbs such as rosemary, rue and thyme could run around the edge to make a picture in the style of an old-fashioned posy. A circular frame in mahogany or oak would finish off the design beautifully.

There are many ideas that could make beautiful herbal gifts using pressed herbs and their flowers. One of the bonuses of pressing is that it takes up very little space compared to drying the herbs or arranging them in their fresh state. So, if space is at a premium for you or for the recipient of your special gift, pressing may well be the answer.

The photograph on p. 34 shows many different herbs, mostly with culinary uses. The pressed collection of wedding flowers in the other photo contains a more aromatic blend of herbs and flowers.

HERBAL MINIATURES

Because herbs are simple unassuming plants, they seem to look better in plain arrangements, without the formality of design that one might use with stronger garden flowers. The selection of miniatures here all have a botanical style to their design. Although executed individually, all the pictures were designed to hang as a set, and the herbs you place in the pictures could depend on your personal favourites or on the choice of the person for whom you are making them.

There are many ideas on which to base a collection. The herbs could all begin with the same letter, such as bay, balm, basil and borage. Alternatively they could all come from the kitchen garden, using thyme, mint, parsley and sage.

The miniature arrangements pictured on pages 38–9 are all on a cream silk back-ground and framed with dainty brass oval and circular frames. The names in both Latin and English were then carefully recorded on the back. There are many small herbs that lend themselves to miniature work.

Although these are a collection of brass frames, you could also frame them in Victorian-style walnut or gilt ovals or rectangular frames, with or without mounts.

Other ideas

Pressed herb greetings cards could make a lovely present if the herb ties in with the gift. For example, you could make a collection of home-made herbal teas with gift tags illustrating the relevant herbs, and a larger card with a collection of all the herbs displayed as a bouquet. A lovely set of writing paper could be made with different herbs decorating each sheet.

See pages 116–17 for more ideas and full instructions on how to make these gifts.

If you are good at calligraphy you could copy out a poem (or compose your own), then decorate it with the relevant pressed flowers, following the list of flower meanings at the back of the book. Favourite family recipes could be written down and decorated with the herbs that appear in them. A sturdier piece of card, or a set of postcards, could be decorated with pressed herbs and a set of recipes written on them for a keen cook. Many home-made cordials and wines can be made with herbal plants, and a set of recipes for them might be very well received.

Once you start thinking along herbal lines, you will have many ideas for unusual presents to delight your family and friends — that is, of course, if you can bear to part with them. Perhaps you should consider making something for yourself first and then, if it works out well, you can make a second version as a present to give away! Hand-made paper looks very attractive, but alternatively there are some very pretty, naturally dyed recycled papers available to give your message a 'green' and environmentally friendly feel, as an added bonus.

These miniature pictures feature many different herbs and related old-fashioned cottage garden flowers. A collection of smaller pictures can sometimes look more effective than one large design as there are more details to enjoy in a small group.

A PRESSED HERBAL WEDDING BOUQUET

Flowers and herbs play a very important part in the celebration of a wedding. As an unusual alternative to traditional wedding flowers, I organized a wedding with a herbal theme recently, where the bride's bouquet and head-dress were mainly flowers and plants with herbal uses. The delphiniums, perhaps, were an exception, but the arrangements still had a herbal/cottage garden feel. They also dried very well — after the wedding the bouquet was dried and the flowers were then wired around a basket filled with pot-pourri. This is a lovely and unusual way of preserving flowers from a wedding or any other special occasion. The bride's head-dress meanwhile was pressed immediately after the wedding, and six weeks later the flowers and herbs were ready for use.

The flowers and herbs included in the picture are delphiniums, feverfew, rue ('Jackman's Blue'), scented geranium leaves, *Adianthum* ferns, wild clematis, *Artemisia* ('Lambrook Silver'), borage flowers, comfrey flowers and conifers.

Apart from looking beautiful as a bouquet and head-dress, the herbs also carry some secret meanings in the language of flowers. In addition to the plants listed above, the bouquet also contained some rosebuds, which mean 'pure and lovely', the scented geraniums mean 'preference', the fern means 'sincerity', borage means 'cheerfulness' (and 'bluntness'!) and the clematis signifies purity. The only meaning I am a little unhappy about is that attributed to rue, which is meant to signify remorse, but I think we'll just ignore that one as it looks so attractive in the design!

Making the design

The design of the picture is really just a recreation of the head-dress, with the delphiniums taking pride of place and small bunches of feverfew tucked in around the circumference. The design is oval, partly because the bride's hairstyle called for it and partly because she asked for the picture to be this shape.

As described for the picture with the mossy green mount, this design was also arranged on silk and then padded before framing. However, it is just as attractive to use a card backing and far easier to frame afterwards! Make sure that all the components are well glued with latex adhesive, as the herbs are very light and can easily move about after framing.

It can look lovely to use home-grown flowers for the bride and attendants. They don't always last as well as bought flowers but while they do the effect is beautiful. A wedding with a country theme can look very natural and helps to make a special day even more so. For example, for the herbal wedding there were pressed flower invitations with a herbal theme, pressed flowers adorned the place cards and the bride and groom also used some notelets decorated with herbal and garden flowers to write their thankyou letters after the wedding.

Fresh Herbs

One of the loveliest ways to use herbs is straight from the garden as fresh flowers and foliage. Although many herbs lack the ostentation of many highly cultivated species, it is in this subtlety of colour that their charm lies. There are many soft hazy shades that all blend together well, but colour co-ordination does not seem so important when using such old-fashioned, charming plants. Just as cottage gardens are ablaze with colour so fresh herbal arrangements can be a joyous selection of all the plants from the herb garden, and they will look wonderful.

FRESH HERBS

Nothing can compare with the gentle aroma of fresh herbs. Whether they are to look beautiful or to be a practical gift, they will be a winner every time! A keen cook would be delighted with some fresh herbs, whether decorating a wreath or planted in a terracotta pot. Gardeners would be interested in a collection of mints or thymes, and anyone would be pleased to receive an arrangement of fresh herbs and flowers.

HERBAL WREATH

An unusual way to give fresh herbs is to attach them to a twig or willow wreath base and add some ribbon or other decoration as the finishing touch. The herbs can then be enjoyed fresh and will dry naturally on the wreath for use in the kitchen or for brewing herbal teas.

A selection of herbs freshly harvested from the garden is a useful asset in the kitchen but is also a very attractive way to decorate the house.

Ingredients

You will need bunches of the following herbs (according to the season):

Rosemary stems
Lavender leaves and stems or flowers, depending on the time of the year
Bay leaves
Lemon verbena
Curry plant
Scented geraniums
Rue
Santolina
Mixed sages
Winter savoury
Mixed thymes

Willow or twig wreath base
Scissors
Fine rose wire
Hot glue gun and supply of glue

Hot glue guns can be purchased from most hardware stores, as can the glue, and they are available in a variety of sizes and qualities. I would recommend buying one of medium quality and medium price, as the larger ones are really only suited to professional use and the smallest varieties are not as tough as I would like.

Carefully wire the different herbs into small bunches and glue the wired stems on to the wreath. To wire a bunch of herbs, take a small clump of herb foliage about 3 in (7.5 cm) long and, with all the stems at the same level, tightly wrap a piece of rose wire around them to hold them together as a bunch. Build up a deliberate or random pattern of ingredients as you wish. Do not use too much glue — placing the glue in one spot only on the wired bunch will enable you or the recipient to cut off carefully small dried

sprigs whenever they are needed. Once you have a pleasing design running around the wreath you can add some narrow ribbons for decoration.

As the herbs dry on the wreath, and you cut pieces off for cooking purposes if you choose to use them, gaps will appear that you can fill with bunches of whichever herbs are in season at that time. If you are giving the wreath away as a present it will be extra special if you add a card listing the uses of the herbs included on the wreath, and perhaps a simple line diagram identifying which herbs are which. The card could be tied on to the wreath with a matching piece of the narrow ribbon. Another idea might be to write out on postcards some favourite recipes or ideas for herbal teas, mentioning all the herbs. If you punch a hole in the top left hand corner of each card, it can be tied to the wreath with a piece of ribbon. A wreath like this takes only a short while to make but would be a lovely gift for a hostess rather than the customary bottle of wine.

PLANTING CONTAINERS WITH HERBS

Many people have very little space in their gardens, or may have nothing bigger than a window box. Here are some lovely gift ideas which I hope will increase the popularity of herbal plants, and that can be kept indoors or in a very small space.

A herbal window box

First you must choose your container. You could buy a ready-made unbreakable plastic window box or make a wooden one

yourself, depending on the time you have available and the skills you wish to make use of.

A terracotta trough blends in with many styles of house. If you are a skilled potter you could even make your own. If you make a window box from wood instead you must treat the wood well with a timber preservative to protect it from the elements.

Most herbs hate waterlogged soil so good drainage is vital. Make sure your chosen container has plenty of drainage holes drilled through its base, then place about 2 in (5 cm) of broken flowerpots or stones in the bottom as a drainage layer. Fill the trough with richer soil than normal garden earth; proprietary brands of herb potting compost can be bought from most garden centres. An organic mix can also be used, made up of:

4 parts good garden soil
3 parts well-rotted garden compost
3 parts moist coconut fibre compost
1 part horticultural sand

Water the soil well and leave to settle before planting up the container. Assuming that the trough is approximately 24 in (60 cm) long, some creeping thymes could be planted at the front to trail over the edges. Other small cuttings from plants such as lavender, rosemary, the scented leaf geraniums, marjoram and parsley all lend themselves well to window boxes.

In many cases the plants have culinary or other uses, so their size will be contained by the frequent trimming of an enthusiastic cook or maker of pot-pourri! The window box will need some regular maintenance to ensure that all the plants have adequate room, and one overly

Here fresh herbs have been used to decorate a circular twig wreath combined with gypsophila and solidaster flowers. The heart-shaped wreath is made from dried lavender stems, and ivy, rue, wax flowers and conifers have been wired on one corner to add a pretty touch without hiding the attractive lavender stems.

enthusiastic specimen is not crowding out all the other inhabitants of the box. It will make a lovely present either for someone with no garden or for a keen gardener or cook who would enjoy having these lovely plants close at hand.

Strawberry pots and other containers

There are many other containers that lend themselves well as presents, but I am only mentioning a few of them here. Once you have decided to plant up an attractive container you can start looking around garden centres, antique shops or even junk shops and jumble sales until inspiration strikes!

Strawberry pots look lovely planted up with attractive herbal foliage poking through each aperture. Smaller plants work best — a collection of various coloured thymes would look stunning or perhaps a selection of different sages. The sage 'Tricolour' is a particularly attractive

plant and would contrast well with a silver grey and purple sage.

Take care to have a good balance of plants in the container, because a large plant on the left-hand side with a much smaller, lighter plant on the right gives the pot a very uncomfortable, wobbly look. You must keep all the plants a roughly similar size and weight to give an even overall balance.

Making a miniature herb garden

An old chipped sink could be put to excellent use as a small herb garden just outside the back door. Although this idea would not win any prizes as the most easily portable gift of the year, it would certainly be very much appreciated. This is the kind of project that many people intend to tackle but never get around to, but it is well worth the effort. Choose some popular culinary herbs, remembering to avoid mint as it will swamp all the other plants in a very short time. Tarragon, basil, parsley and nasturtiums would make a good splash of colour and would all be

useful so near the kitchen. Alternatively, you could choose herbal plants that you know the recipient loves, such as lavenders or flowering herbs, to give a pretty and colourful look to this miniature garden.

A half-barrel can look very effective filled with bushy and trailing herbs. Of course, it is not a very practical present if you are travelling to the recipient's house by train, but assuming you would not find the transport a problem, and you do not choose a large barrel, this is an unusual idea that would be well received.

A herbal tea garden

A selection of herbs that are particularly useful for herbal teas would make an unusual theme for a collection of plants. If they were given with full details of how to infuse the leaves or flowers and what ills they help to ease, they could make a

The mint family are amongst the most popular herbs and this variegated apple mint looks beautiful in the garden and has many uses once it has been picked.

present with a difference. As well as the planted container and instructions you could even give a suitable teapot or infuser and an especially beautiful china cup and saucer!

To make teas with fresh herbs, use three teaspoons per cup and, for dried herbs, use one teaspoon for each cup. These are some of the most useful teas, but further details can be found on page 28. Basil, bergamot, camomile, catmint, comfrey, heather, fennel, hops, hyssop, lemon balm, caraway, sweet cicely, lovage, meadow-sweet, mint, parsley, rosemary, sage, salad burnet, thyme and vervain, feverfew and lungwort.

Herbal teas have been used for many centuries as remedies for many maladies, and even if they are just used as a delicious drink they are well worth some time and experimentation.

USING A COLOUR THEME

Often a colour may be a useful link to inspire your choice of herbs for a present. If you want a completely different idea for a golden or silver wedding anniversary present, herbs might just be the answer.

Silver herb gardens

With a silver wedding present in mind, keep to silvers and greys and you will have a soft colour selection that would blend in with any patio or spot in the garden. There are several possibilities but these plants could form a basis for your collection:

Cotton lavender (*Santolina chaemcyparissus*)
Curry plant (*Helichrysum angustifolium*)

Lavenders (perhaps pink, white and blue varieties)
Rosemary (there are several kinds to choose from)
Silver thyme (*Thymus citriodorus*)
Wormwood (*Artemisia absinthium* 'Lambrook Silver') or southernwood (*Artemisia abrotanum*)

Golden herb gardens

There are also many plants to choose from for a golden wedding group, and bearing in mind that couples celebrating their golden wedding anniversaries have collected many things for their home already, they may be very grateful for such an unusual and practical gift.

Marigold (*Calendula officinalis*)
Dyers camomile (*Anthemis tinctoria*)
Curry plant (*Helichrysum angustifolium*)
Golden bay (*Laurus nobilis* 'Aureum')
Golden marjoram (*Origanum vulgare* 'Aureum')
Cotton lavender (*Santolina chamaecyparissus*)
Golden sage (*Salvia officinalis* 'Icterina')
French marigold (*Tagetes patula*)
Tansy (*Tanacetum vulgare*)
Golden thyme (*Thymus* 'Doone Valley')

This makes an unusual golden gift, and one that can be enjoyed for many months or more, rather than just the few days that fresh flowers last.

Other ideas

You could also base your scheme on a personal choice of colour, perhaps picking your friend's favourite colours: one example here is a combination of purple and gold. Alternatively you could choose pink and grey, green and white, or cream, but

there are several possibilities once you think along these lines.

Here are some suggestions for a purple and gold colour scheme:

Purple basil (*Ocimum basilicum*)
Red sage (*Salvia officinalis* 'Purpurescens')
Eau-de-Cologne mint (*Mentha citrata*)
Feverfew (*Chrysanthemum parthenium*)
Golden marjoram (*Origanum vulgare* 'Aureum')
Golden thyme (*Thymus vulgaris* 'Aureum')

The contrast of the dark basil against the brighter golds is very striking.

INDOOR HERB POTS

Most people can find a small space on their kitchen window sill for some pots of herbs. By growing them indoors, the season for such tender annuals as basil and summer savoury can be extended and, of course, they are always within easy reach whenever they are needed.

An attractive terracotta pot planted up with a single variety of herb would be a lovely gift, or a larger container with a selection of herbs for people with plenty of space. When thinking of a present for a family member or close friend (when you know it will be well received), you could design an indoor herb garden around a kitchen or other suitable window. It must be a sunny and draught-free position and preferably receiving full sun (the herbs will go leggy and pale in deep shade). Even if the window sill space is limited, more room could be found by adding a narrow shelf halfway up the window. This looks decorative as well as being practical.

Many plants that are ideal for indoor herb gardening are very easily and cheaply raised from seed or cuttings, so the major outlay for this gift idea would be your time and effort rather than your money. Try to find a particularly attractive container as it makes an enormous difference to the final appearance of the gift; a rather dull plastic container with a semi-healthy specimen inside it won't raise more than a half-hearted thank you. On the other hand, a really unusual, perhaps even antique, terracotta container filled with a flourishing clump of vivid green parsley, or whichever herb you decide upon, will be received with true appreciation.

Culinary herbs
Many culinary herbs are quite happy growing indoors, and there are many pretty colours and shapes to choose from. The variegated forms are a good contrast to the stronger greens and darker tones. Here are some ideas from which to make your selection:

Basil (*Ocimum basilicum*)
Coriander (*Coriandrum sativum*)
Thymes (*Thymus* sp.)
Winter and summer savourys (*Satureia* sp.)
Sage (*Salvia officinalis*)
Rosemary (*Rosmarinus officinalis*)
Lemon verbena (*Aloysia triphylla*)
Scented geraniums (*Pelargonium* sp.)
Sages (*Salvia* sp.)
Chervil (*Anthriscus cerefolium*)
Chives (*Allium schoenoprasum*)
Marjoram (*Origanum vulgare*)
Parsley (*Petroselinum crispum*)

The larger varieties, such as lemon verbena, would be better in a pot of their own, and the more invasive herbs, such as mint,

should be kept apart from other herbs as they will take over in a mixed pot. The pots or containers could be plain terra-cotta or stencilled to co-ordinate with a particular colour scheme. Perhaps some china plant pot holders could link up with the colour scheme of the room.

FRESH HERBS IN POSIES AND TUSSIE-MUSSIES

A tussie-mussie is a fragrant herbal posy that was carried in days gone by as a natural deodorizing accessory. Conditions on city streets would have been close to intolerable at times because sanitation was practically non-existent. Not only would the streets have smelt disgusting, but the people walking along them would not have been much better. Bathing was far from a daily occurrence, and anyone bathing once a month would have considered themselves oustandingly clean, because many people didn't wash at all! Not surprisingly, disease was rampant, so it was hoped that the antiseptic qualities of some plants warded off germs as well as smells. Clutching a sweet-smelling nosegay must have been far preferable to the ambient aroma!

Very aromatic plants should be mixed in a posy with care as one strong fragrance may cancel out or overpower another. Try instead to choose plants that will blend both in colour and fragrance, so you create a posy with a pleasing smell and shape. During Victorian times, these posies also incorporated messages using the language of flowers, and you could copy this idea to give a theme to a bouquet for a

special occasion. A Mother's Day posy could include some of the following herbs and flowers to add an extra dimension to a pretty posy.

African violet Such worth is rare
Coltsfoot Maternal care
Sage Esteem
Rosemary Remembrance
Camomile Patience
Alchemilla Protection
'Doris' pinks Love

Fresh posies can make a refreshing change as a gift when you are visiting friends. Providing the posy is put in water as soon as possible on arrival, it should last about a week. A fine cook might appreciate a posy of edible herbs, if not to use that night then for cooking with at a later date.

Making a herbal posy or tussie-mussie

Choose your material carefully from the garden and then place it in a deep vase with plenty of water to make sure the herbs have a really good drink. Once they have had a chance to take up some water you can start work.

Choose a single rose or fairly impressive single flower as a centrepiece. Alternatively, if there is a central theme to the message contained in the bouquet then a cluster of that ingredient might make a good central feature. Trim the central flower or small bunch of flowers to the length required — usually the depth of your fist — and tie

Fresh posies are very simple to create. Simply bind bunches of herbs around a central flower (in this case a red rose), then add more ingredients until the posy is the size you require.

well together with florist's tape. Gradually add in the other ingredients in concentric rings, taking care to have a pleasing choice of shapes, sizes and colours next to each other. Finish with an outer ring of a fairly frothy or delicate plant to give the effect of a frill or ruff. Alternatively, a pale lace frill can be attached instead. Once the bouquet is firmly taped, you can trim all the stalks and decorate with toning ribbons.

FRESH FLOWER ARRANGEMENTS WITH HERBS

At the height of summer there is nothing lovelier than an armful of fragrant roses and herbs. Bringing them into the house lifts one's spirits and brings a smile to the face of everyone who sees them. Natural styles of arrangement are prettiest, using soft herb materials rather than rigid old-fashioned triangular displays. There are very few people who would not be thrilled to receive a fresh herb arrange-ment; the combination of a lovely smell and something beautiful to look at is always successful. Try arranging old-fashioned roses with *Alchemilla mollis*, sweet cicely leaves and stems of rosemary. Not only will the arrangement look lovely but it will lightly scent the whole room.

Many containers are useful for arranging herbal flowers but simple styles and uncluttered designs work best. Rustic containers and plain lines show the plants to their best advantage and don't distract the eye. Try picking a random selection of everything that looks attractive in the herb garden at that particular moment. That is not customary advice for flower arrangers, but it can work when picking herbs as they are all fairly gentle plants and blend well together. Subtle colour mixes of cream, grey and silver are easily achieved with herbal selections, and the cottage garden style is very effectively transferred indoors.

Table arrangements

As well as larger flower arrangements with herbs, you could try some miniature designs. Small designs beside each place at the dining table give each guest a pretty arrangement to appreciate and take home. When arranged in this way, the aromas can be less overpowering than a large display in the centre of the table. As an alternative, small bunches of herbs could be tied up with ribbons and placed on each napkin. Including unusual herbs makes a good talking point and means the gifts are extra special.

Winter herbal ideas

Fresh herbs can feature in gifts and arrangements all year round. When you are working on decorations or arrange-ments as gifts for Christmas, you could include bay leaves or rosemary in your designs. A Christmas table centre would look lovely with thick ivory candles and a collection of rosemary, bay, myrtle, cotton lavender, curry plant, rue and some scented geraniums. Apart from making one for your own home, why not make one for a sister or good friend — it would be a very welcome gift at such a busy festive time.

Herbs also smell gorgeous when they are burnt on an open fire. Pine cones are often used but you could try bundles of lavender stalks or stems of rosemary

instead. If you edge a basket with flowers and herbs and then fill it with pine cones and bundles of lavender stems, it makes a very unusual present that would grace any fireplace. A similar idea could be used in the summer months — a basket to keep by the barbecue, filled with sprigs of rosemary and lavender, wood chips and other scented herbs, could be edged with some herb sprays and ribbons.

Herbs for weddings
Weddings are another time of great celebration and can benefit from a herbal influence. Using fresh herbs instead of paper confetti can be appreciated, as long as the herbs are cut up small enough and mixed with scented rose petals. The herbs can also be dried and made into natural confetti. There is a certain romance about using fresh rose petals: any couple would be thrilled to have the pretty mixture, suggested below, strewn before them or over them as they leave the church or reception.

All the ingredients should be freshly picked:

½ pint (300 ml) chopped lemon verbena leaves
¼ pint (150 ml) individual dill flowers
½ pint (300 ml) borage flowers
½ pint (300 ml) clove pink petals
1 pint (600 ml) rose petals, pink or red
½ pint (300 ml) myrtle leaves

The messages hidden within these flowers include love (myrtle and pinks) and pure and lovely (roses), so although it's a little one-track minded it seems to send the right message! The recipe can be altered to suit the quantity of confetti that you wish to make and the ingredients available.

The fresh flower confetti could be packed into small bags and trimmed with ribbons, then given to several of the wedding guests to throw over the bride and groom. Alternatively, you could just throw fresh rose petals over the happy couple. This looks and smells lovely and is also bio-degradeable, unlike some of the commercial confetti available today.

HERBS IN THE KITCHEN

Herbs really come into their own in the kitchen. They have been used in cookery for thousands of years, and the Romans had many herbs that they relied upon heavily, such as anise, basil, bay, capers, coriander, cumin and dill. The list goes on and on, so herbal flavouring is far from new. However, there has been a resurgence of interest in the use of fresh herbs recently and today they are widely available in most supermarkets and grocery stores. Food is always a welcome gift, especially home-made delicacies, so here are a few recipes to set you thinking along the right lines.

GIVING FOOD AS GIFTS

When giving an edible gift, packaging is of paramount importance. Clear labelling is tremendously helpful, so the recipient knows exactly what the gift contains and also how to keep it fresh. If there are refrigeration instructions then make sure they are easily read or your hard work may go off overnight!

There are a great many possibilities for herbal food, but one broad generalization is that fresh herbs taste better than dried ones. If a particular ingredient is not available fresh you can substitute the dried version instead, but I would suggest that you choose another recipe as the taste of fresh herbs is much more subtle and pleasing than that of dried.

Collections of various foods make a very attractive gift and can be quite simple — a basket of jams and jellies, or a collection of herbal oils and vinegars, make marvellous presents. To avoid mistakes, it is best to tailor your gift to the tastes of the recipient. If he or she is particularly keen on vegetarian foods, then perhaps a set of special sauces for use with pasta and vegetables would be well received.

Pretty bottles or baskets help the presentation look much more attractive. A gaily checked cloth lining a simple basket would make a lovely foil for some herbal breads, and such an unusual present would be sure to please.

Some of the herbal recipes in this chapter are shown here packaged as gifts. Breads, cheeses and pâtés are always popular presents.

PÂTÉS AND MOUSSES

Pâtés are always a popular lunchtime snack or first course for an evening meal. There are many variations on this theme and the following suggestions are recipes that I have found particularly successful. Don't despair if you don't have a food processor — you can mince the ingredients, or pound them with a pestle and mortar and then use a blender. Make sure you attach labels to the finished items, stating that they must be kept in the fridge and also a date by which they should be eaten. There are very smart containers available at kitchen shops in all manner of finishes, but an inexpensive range is available in pure white, which looks very effective. The pâté could be packed into a ramekin or loaf tin, and a sample selection of pâtés, all in individual ramekins in a basket lined with a brightly coloured napkin, would look lovely.

An unusual way to package a fish mousse would be to keep it in the fish-shaped mould that it was made in. There are some beautiful copper moulds available, and for a keen cook this would be a present that could be used time and time again. If you give enough thought to the problem, there are always new and different ways to wrap a food parcel to give it a touch of originality.

Potted shrimps

4 oz (100 g) unsalted butter
12 oz (350 g) shrimps (cooked)
1 tbsp (15 ml) lemon juice
¼ tsp (1.25 g) cayenne pepper
salt and pepper to taste
1 tsp (5 g) chopped lemon balm

Melt 3 oz (75 g) of the butter in a pan and

remove from the heat. Skim the foam off the top of the butter and discard. Add the shrimps, lemon juice, cayenne, lemon balm and seasonings to the melted butter, mix well and divide between two large ramekin dishes. Melt the remaining butter and again remove the foam from the top. Pour the remaining butter — taking care not to include any sediment – over the shrimps. Chill in the fridge overnight. These potted shrimps will keep for several weeks in the refrigerator.

Ideas for packaging: wrap well with foil or cling film and decorate with ribbons; or place on a tray with some cheese and herb scones (see page 81).

Salmon and dill mousse

2 × 7oz (200 g) cans pink salmon
3 tbsp (45 ml) mayonnaise
1 chicken stock cube
2 tbsp (30 ml) double cream
1 sachet gelatine
1 egg white
1 tbsp (15 g) chopped dill leaves

Mix the salmon and mayonnaise together in a bowl. In a jug, add a tablespoon (15 ml) of boiling water to the stock cube, add the juice from the cans of salmon and mix in the gelatine. When it has melted, add the cream and stir well. Add the gelatine liquid to the salmon mixture and combine well. Whisk the egg white until stiff, add the dill and fold into the mixture. Fill six individual ramekins or a salmon-shaped mould with the mixture.

Ideas for presentation: once the mousse is thoroughly chilled, it can be decorated with cucumber or dill leaves. To present the mousse, line a basket with dark blue tissue paper, then add the large mousse or individual ones, tightly wrapped in cling film, plus a bottle of home-made dill mayonnaise. A nice extra would be a bottle of dry white wine to drink with it!

Chicken liver and herb pâté

1 lb (450 g) chicken livers
2 tbsp (30 g) chopped onion
5 oz (150 g) butter
2 fl oz (50 ml) medium sherry
1 fl oz (25 ml) cream
salt and pepper
1 tbsp (15 g) mixed, chopped fresh herbs
  (including marjoram, parsley, thyme or chives)

Melt 1 oz (25 g) of the butter in a frying pan, fry the onions and then the chicken livers until they are just cooked. Place in the bowl of a food processor. Melt the rest of the butter and add to the chicken livers. Then place all the remaining ingredients in the bowl and process until smooth. Pour into small ramekins or other dishes if you prefer.

Ideas for presentation: a small hamper containing small pots of the chicken and herb pâté, an airtight tin filled with melba toast, and some good red wine.

Smoky cod and ginger pâté

1 lb (450 g) smoked cod
5 oz (150 g) butter
¾ tsp (3.5 g) grated fresh ginger
1 tbsp (15 ml) double cream
salt and pepper to taste

Poach the fish until tender. Once the fish is cool place it in a food processor with all the other ingredients and process until well combined and smooth. Press the mixture into a lined loaf tin or other container and chill in the fridge overnight.

Idea for presentation: fill several small containers and put them into a basket with some home-made rolls and a few lemons.

Potted Cheshire cheese and chives

3 oz (75g) unsalted butter
8 oz (225 g) Cheshire cheese
2 tbsp (30 ml) port
dash of Worcestershire sauce
1 tbsp (15 g) chopped chives
1 tbsp (15 ml) Greek yoghurt
pinch of cayenne pepper
chopped chives to garnish

Process all the ingredients in a blender or food processor and spoon into individual ramekins. Chill and garnish with chives.

Idea for presentation: pack in a box or basket lined with a red-spotted handkerchief, and add some Bath Oliver biscuits and some pickles.

Pots of pâté are easily wrapped or packaged to make an unusual gift. Inexpensive containers can be collected throughout the year in readiness for Christmas or other special occasions.

Hummus with mint and parsley

15 oz (425 g) can chick peas
1–2 cloves garlic, crushed
4 tbsp (60 g) tahini (sesame paste)
2 tbsp (30 ml) olive oil
3 tbsp (45 ml) lemon juice
½ tsp (2.5 g) cumin, ground
salt and pepper to taste
2–3 tbsp (30–45 ml) Greek-style yoghurt
1 tbsp (15 g) chopped parsley
1 tbsp (15 g) chopped mint

Put the chick peas in a blender or food processor, add the garlic, tahini, oil, lemon juice and seasonings. Blend until smooth. Add the yoghurt, mint and parsley and blend again. Spoon the mixture into ramekins and decorate with sprigs of parsley.

Idea for presentation: arrange the ramekins on a bed of clean straw in a basket and add some wholemeal pitta bread and a bottle of alcoholic or non-alcoholic refreshment, then cover with cellophane and a large ribbon.

Courgette pâté

9 oz (250 g) courgettes, sliced
salt and pepper
1 tsp (5 g) fresh rosemary
1 tbsp (15 g) fresh chives
5 oz (150 g) full-fat soft cheese

Process the herbs in a food processor until finely chopped. Add the courgettes and process together. Add the cheese and process until well mixed, then add salt and pepper to taste. Turn into one large dish or several small ones and chill.

Idea for presentation: this is a lovely pâté

for a vegetarian, so wrap with other vegetarian delights (see cheeses or herbs with vegetables) and a spray of fresh herbs.

Potted chicken

4 oz (100 g) butter
1 onion, finely chopped
1–2 cloves garlic, chopped
8 oz (225 g) chicken meat, finely chopped
2 tbsp (30 ml) medium sherry
4 tbsp (60 ml) chicken stock
salt and pepper
pinch of nutmeg
pinch of mixed herbs, dried

Melt half the butter in a frying pan, add the onion and garlic and fry for 5 minutes until soft. Add all the other ingredients and stir well. Fill four ramekin dishes with the mixture and chill in the refrigerator until firm. Melt the remaining butter and pour a thin layer over each ramekin.

Ideas for presentation: this would be attractive in a 'chicken-theme' basket. Line the basket and arrange the ramekins inside, then add some new-laid eggs and a jar of really good home-made chicken stock. If your artistic talents stretch that far, the label could be in the shape of a chicken, but if you feel that is beyond you, how about the shape of an egg!

HERBS ON A PICNIC

Everyone loves a picnic, and here are some ideas that will transform an *al fresco* meal into a feast, especially if they are given as a present.

Gammon cooked in cider and sage

3 lb (1.3 kg) gammon
2 pints (1.2 l) cider
6–8 cloves, plus extra for decoration
bouquet garni
1 tbsp (15 g) sage, dried
2 tbsp (30 g) brown sugar

Soak the gammon overnight to reduce its saltiness. Place the gammon in a large saucepan, add the cider to cover, plus the cloves, sage and bouquet garni. Bring to the boil and then cover and simmer for 1¼ hours, turning the meat occasionally. When the gammon is cooked, strip off the skin but leave a layer of fat. Place the joint in a roasting pan, score a diamond pattern over it and decorate with brown sugar and more cloves. Bake in a hot oven — 425°F (220°C) or Gas Mark 7 — for 15–20 minutes until the outside is brown and crispy.

The gammon makes a lovely centrepiece for the hamper shown overleaf, and is always a welcome present, especially at holiday times when extra guests are being catered for.

Chicken with mango and mint

1 large 3–4 lb (1.3–1.8 kg) roasting chicken
handful of fresh mint
3 tbsp (45 ml) mayonnaise
1 tbsp (15 g) mango purée
1 tbsp (15 g) mango chutney
1 tbsp (15 ml) whipped cream
1 tbsp (15 g) fresh mint

Place the cleaned chicken in a roasting pan and add 1–1½ in (2.5–4 cm) of water around the bird. Place some fresh mint in the water and in the cavity of the chicken. Roast in a hot oven — 425°F (220°C) or Gas Mark 7 — for about one hour or until a skewer pushed into the flesh leaves a trail of clear liquid. Leave to cool, then cut the flesh from the bones and chop roughly. Mix all the other ingredients in a food processor and once the chicken is cool mix into the mango mayonnaise. Pack into a shallow dish and garnish with pieces of mango or sprigs of mint.

Tarragon fish with avocado

1½ lb (675 g) cod or haddock fillets
1 large ripe avocado
lemon juice
1 tbsp (15 g) chopped fresh tarragon
salt and pepper to taste
melted butter
tarragon to garnish
24 sheets filo pastry

Remove all the skin and bones from the fillets and cut into 12 strips. Cut the

A food hamper is always a lovely present, and here the ingredients are assembled for a wonderful picnic. A beautifully decorated cardboard box or orange box can be just as effective.

avocado into 12 wedges and sprinkle both the fish and avocado with lemon juice before placing on separate plates. Brush one sheet of filo pastry with melted butter and place a second on top. Fold them in half and butter the top, then place two strips of fish and two of avocado in the corner, sprinkle with a little tarragon and fold the pastry over, fold in the sides and brush with butter. Finish wrapping the parcel and place it on a greased baking sheet with the join side down. Wrap the other five parcels in the same way and cook at 325°F (170°C), Gas Mark 3 for 18–20 minutes.

Scotch eggs with sage

5 eggs (size 3)
1 oz (25 g) plain flour
salt and pepper to taste
8 oz (225 g) pork sausagemeat
2 oz (50 g) wholemeal breadcrumbs, toasted
½ tsp (2.5 g) dried sage

Hard-boil four of the eggs and leave to cool in cold water. Season the flour with salt and pepper. Work the dried sage into the sausagemeat, then divide into four. Using a floured board, work each piece into a circle large enough to cover an egg. Lightly dust the eggs with the seasoned flour, then place one egg in the centre of each piece of sausagemeat. Mould the sausagemeat around the eggs and then pinch the edges to seal them firmly together.

Beat the remaining egg and use it to coat the Scotch eggs, then roll them in breadcrumbs. Deep-fry the Scotch eggs for about eight minutes until crisp and brown. Leave to cool.

Packing the picnic hamper

There are many other possibilities that you could include in a presentation hamper similar to the one illustrated. Apart from the meat suggestions here you could add jars of pickles and jellies (the recipes are featured later in this chapter). Giving a mixture of goodies that the recipient will like best is the main aim. You could also add some non-food herbal ideas, such as a small tussie-mussie (see Chapter Three) or some herbal teas.

Really beautiful hampers can be hard to find, so a large basket could be used instead or even a big cardboard box covered in an attractive paper or some cotton fabric. Add plenty of ribbon and large labels for a really extravagant effect and what will be a very memorable present.

HERBAL JAMS AND JELLIES

Herbal preserves and jellies are very simple to make, taste wonderful and are very useful and unusual gifts. Some herbal jellies are well-known, mint jelly being one of the best examples. Others, although less famous, are equally delicious when eaten with a variety of meats and poultry. Another bonus is that jams and jellies last well and can therefore be made well in advance. Better still, a store of them can be accumulated when the ingredients are in season and then you will always have a hostess gift in stock.

Although the following recipes mention specific herbs, there are many possible variations on this theme. Using apple jelly as a base, you can add many different herbs to the apple: for example, you could combine apple and rosemary, apple and mint or apple and thyme. The possibilities are only limited by the number of jars you can collect and the ingredients that you have available (not to mention the time you may or may not have!)

Lemon and mint marmalade

8 medium lemons, well scrubbed
4 pints (2.4 l) water
4 lb (1.8 kg) granulated sugar
8 tbsp (120 g) fresh mint

Halve the lemons, remove the pips, then squeeze the juice into a large bowl. Chop the peel fairly small and add to the bowl. Place the lemon pips in a small muslin bag and put in the bowl with the other ingredients. Boil the water, add to the bowl and leave to infuse for 48 hours, covered with a cloth.

Empty the contents of the bowl into a preserving pan and simmer gently for approximately one hour. Warm the sugar in a basin in the oven. Remove the muslin bag of pips from the preserving pan and add the warmed sugar. Stir until it has dissolved, then bring to the boil and allow to boil rapidly for ten minutes.

Remove from the heat. Wash the mint thoroughly and chop finely. Add the mint to the pan and stir well. Pour into clean, warm jars and cover immediately with circles of waxed paper. Once the marmalade has cooled, cover each jar with cellophane and add a label.

Apple and elderflower jam

3 lb (1.3 kg) cooking apples
½ pint (275 ml) water
8 heads of elderflowers, fresh
2 lb (900 g) sugar

Peel and core the apples and place them in a preserving pan with the elderflowers and the water. Simmer gently until the apples are soft. Add the sugar and stir until it has dissolved. Bring the jam to the boil and allow to boil rapidly until it reaches setting point. (If using a thermometer, setting point is at 221° F [105° C]. If not, spoon a little jam on to a chilled saucer, allow to cool and then push your finger across its surface — it will wrinkle when it has reached setting point.) Remove the elderflowers and then pour the jam into warm, clean jars and cover each one with a circle of waxed paper. Once the jam has cooled, cover each jar with cellophane and add a label.

Damson and rose petal jam

3 lb (1.3 kg) damsons
12 large scented roses, pink or dark red
2½ lb (1.1 kg) granulated sugar
4 tbsp (60 ml) water

Pull the roses apart and discard the centres and stems. Trim the white part from the base of each petal. Wash the petals and tear into small pieces.

Wash the damsons well and remove the stones. Place the damsons in a preserving pan and add the rose petals and water.

Home-made jams and jellies are a special gift that pleases anyone. Making a simple herb jelly takes relatively little time and gives so much pleasure.

Simmer gently for approximately 30 minutes, stirring regularly. Warm the sugar in the oven.

Add the warmed sugar to the damson mixture and stir until it has dissolved. Boil for about 15 minutes, stirring constantly to prevent the rose petals falling to the bottom of the mixture. Remove from the heat and allow to cool for five minutes, then stir well and pour into warm clean jars and cover each one with a waxed paper disc. Once the jam has cooled, cover each jar with cellophane and add a label.

Gooseberry and lemon balm jelly

4 lb (1.8 kg) eating apples, peeled and
  chopped
2 lb (900 g) gooseberries
2 tbsp (30 ml) lemon juice
3 tbsp (45 g) chopped lemon balm
1½ pints (900 ml) water
granulated sugar

Place the apples, lemon juice, gooseberries, water and 1 tbsp (15 g) of lemon balm in a large pan. Cover with a lid and bring to the boil. Reduce the heat and then simmer the mixture for about 30 minutes. Ladle the mixture into a jelly bag or piece of fine muslin and allow to drip through into a bowl for 24 hours.

Measure the liquid that has passed through the jelly bag and, for every pint (600 ml) of liquid add 1 lb (450 g) of sugar. Simmer in a preserving pan until the sugar has dissolved, then boil rapidly for 10–15 minutes. Allow to cool for five minutes and stir in the remaining lemon balm. Pour into warm, clean jars and cover with waxed circles of paper. Once the jam has cooled, cover and label as before.

Mint and apple jelly

3 lb (1.3 kg) cooking apples, peeled and
* chopped*
1 lemon, quartered
2 pints (1.2 l) water
large handful of mint, finely chopped
2 tsp (10 g) cider vinegar
granulated sugar

Place the apples, lemons, cider vinegar
and water in a preserving pan and simmer
for 45 minutes until the fruit is soft. Strain
through a jelly bag or piece of muslin
overnight.

Measure the amount of liquid that has
passed through the jelly bag and add 1 lb
(450 g) of sugar for every pint (600 ml) of
liquid. Add the fresh mint and boil this
mixture in a preserving pan for 15 minutes,
stirring occasionally. Remove from the
heat and leave to stand for ten minutes. As
an optional extra you can add a little more
chopped mint at this stage. Then pour into
warm, clean jars, cover with waxed paper
circles and leave to cool. Once cool, cover
each jar with cellophane and add a label.

Scented geranium jelly

6 lb (2.6 kg) eating apples
50 lemon-scented geranium leaves
2 pints (1.2 l) water
granulated sugar

Place the chopped apples, washed geranium
leaves and water in a preserving pan. Bring
to the boil and simmer for 45 minutes.
Ladle into a jelly bag or piece of muslin
and allow to drip through overnight.

Measure the liquid and add 1 lb (450 g)
of sugar for every pint (600 ml) of liquid.
Simmer in a preserving pan until the sugar

dissolves, then boil rapidly for ten minutes.
Remove from the heat, pour into clean,
warm jars and cover with waxed circles of
paper. When cool, cover each jar with
cellophane and add a label.

Rose jelly

4 lb (1.8 kg) green apples
2 pints (1.2 l) water
6 large scented pink or red roses
rosewater
granulated sugar

Place the apples and water in a pan and
simmer for about 45 minutes until soft.
Strain the liquid through a jelly bag
overnight.

Measure the strained liquid and add 1 lb
(450 g) of sugar for every pint (600 ml) of
liquid. Place in a preserving pan and
simmer well until the sugar has dissolved.
Remove the petals from five of the roses
and cut the white parts off the base of the
petals. Add to the pan and bring to the
boil. Boil rapidly for ten minutes, then
remove all the rose petals with a perforated
spoon.

Add the petals from the last rose
(having removed all the white parts from
the base of the petals), plus about eight
drops of rosewater, and stir. Pour into
clean warm jars and cover with waxed
paper circles. Once cool, cover each jar
with cellophane and add a label.

Packaging jams and jellies

The easiest way to decorate a present of
jams and jellies is to give each jar a fabric
or paper hat. There are many suitable
materials to choose from: plain or coloured
paper, white or metallic doilies, antique

linen or lace handkerchiefs, plain or printed fabrics.

Using pinking shears gives a better finish and will prevent the material fraying. A 6-in (15-cm) circle will fit the top of most jam jars, but do measure the size you need and cut it accordingly. Centre the circle of fabric over the top of the jam jar and hold it place with an elastic band. Then cover the elastic band with ribbon or lace, cord or even coloured shoe laces for fun!

Try to match the fabric to the contents of the jar; for example, a rose petal jelly could have a pale pink taffeta hat and a lace bow. A garden herb jelly could have a recycled paper hat and garden twine to secure the cover. A strong presentation with plain or checked primary-coloured fabric, secured with brightly coloured shoe laces, would look very striking, perhaps on some damson jam or on one of the pickles or chutneys.

MUSTARDS

Mustards are delicious, and give a lift to all sorts of savoury foods. We all know the English, French and German varieties, but these recipes give them an extra lift and would make marvellous presents for a mustard lover.

Minty mustard

1 × 8 oz (225 g) jar wholegrain coarse
 mustard
4 tsp (20 g) dry mint leaves, finely crumbled

Mix these two ingredients well and either return the mixture to the original jar or put it in smaller jars to give as part of a set of small mustards.

Tarragon mustard with vermouth

large handful fresh tarragon leaves
4 oz (100 g) chopped spring onions
2 × 8 oz (225 g) jars Dijon mustard
1 tbsp (15 ml) dry vermouth

Chop the tarragon leaves well and add the spring onions, mustard and vermouth. Mix together very thoroughly. Pour into a clean jar and seal with a tight-fitting lid. This mustard can be stored in the refrigerator for about one month.

PICKLES

Pickles can add their own special zing to a meal and are particularly good with cold cuts of meat or poultry. Most vegetables will pickle, so here are some recipes that are especially good.

Dilly cucumbers

24 small ridge cucumbers
5 pints (3 l) water
1/2 pint (300 ml) vinegar
4 oz (100 g) sea salt
1 large handful fresh dill heads
1 large or several small chilli peppers

Soak the cucumbers overnight in a solution of salt and water, using 8 oz (225 g) of sea salt to every pint (600 ml) of water. Then boil together the water, vinegar and sea salt and allow to cool. Drain the cucumbers and arrange in clean Kilner jars interspersed with layers of dill heads. The cucumbers can be left whole or cut into slices. Add a small chilli pepper or pieces of a larger one to each jar. Cover with the vinegar solution and secure the lids.

It takes only seconds to place some pieces of herb or spice into bottles of oil or vinegar and, with an attractive bottle, you have a lovely gift in moments.

Sweet pickled onions

2 lb (900 g) pickling onions
1 bunch tarragon
1 bunch mint
1 bunch sweet cicely
4 oz (100 g) sea salt
1 pint (600 ml) cider vinegar
6 oz (175 g) granulated sugar

Peel the onions then arrange them on a tray, sprinkle with the sea salt and leave overnight. Carefully wipe all the salt and moisture off the onions and place in clean jars. Put a couple of sprigs of each herb in every jar. Heat the vinegar and sugar until the sugar is completely dissolved, then leave to cool. Pour the vinegar over the onions, leaving a very small amount of room in the top of each jar. Secure the lids of the jars. The onions will be ready in about two to three weeks but are a lot tastier after about six to eight weeks, if you can wait that long!

Mint and tomato chow chow

6 average tomatoes
1 onion
1 green pepper, chopped
2 tbsp (30 g) brown sugar
1 tbsp (15 g) salt
½ pint (300 ml) cider vinegar
2 tbsp (30 g) finely chopped mint

Peel the tomatoes by placing them in boiling water for a few seconds and then carefully removing the skins. Peel the onion and chop the tomatoes and onion finely. Put all the ingredients in a lidded casserole dish and cook at 300°F (150°C), Gas Mark 2, until the onion is quite tender (about one to two hours). Remove from the oven and leave to cool. Pour into wide-mouthed jars and cover each jar with a circle of waxed paper, then cover with cellophane and add a label.

Mint relish

1 pint (600 ml) mint leaves
1 lb (450 g) onions, peeled and chopped
1 lb (450 g) apples, peeled and chopped
½ lb (225 g) green tomatoes, peeled and
  chopped
1 lb (450 g) sultanas
2 tsp (10 g) salt
2 tsp (10 g) French mustard
1 pint (600 ml) white wine vinegar
1 lb (450 g) granulated sugar

Heat ¼ pint (150 ml) of vinegar with the sugar until the sugar has completely dissolved. Leave to cool. Place the remaining vinegar in a saucepan with the salt and mustard. Put the green tomatoes in a food processor for a few seconds until they are mushy, then add to the saucepan. Repeat the process with the mint leaves, apples, onions and sultanas, adding them all to the saucepan. Then simmer all the ingredients until soft. Pour in the vinegar and sugar mixture. Boil the mixture for a couple of minutes and then leave to cool a little. Pour the relish into warm clean jars and cover with waxed paper circles. When completely cool, add cellophane lids and labels.

SAUCES

Sauces make a very unusual gift. Although you must provide clear labelling to indicate whether they need to be refrigerated or not, a basket containing a selection of sauces could be very welcome, especially at Christmas. At a time when plenty of ingenuity is needed to use up the inevitable leftovers, a Christmas gift of delicious and unusual sauces could be a real winner!

Pesto

This very Italian sauce is delicious with many foods, as well as pasta. Mixed with mayonnaise it makes a lovely sauce for cold turkey, or you could use it when stuffing some tiny tomatoes or mushrooms. Although you need fresh basil for this recipe, once it has been made the sauce lasts in the fridge for at least a month or freezes indefinitely.

1 lb (450 g) fresh sweet basil leaves
4 oz (100 g) parsley
8 garlic cloves, peeled and chopped
8 oz (225 g) pine nuts
3/4 pint (450 ml) virgin olive oil
8 oz (225 g) Parmesan cheese
sea salt and pepper

Combine the basil, parsley, garlic and pine nuts in a food processor. Process until the mixture resembles a coarse paste. Slowly add the olive oil in a steady stream, with the processor switched on, until all the oil is used up. Add the cheese, sea salt and coarsely ground black pepper and process again for a couple of seconds. Depending on how you plan to package your gift, scrape the mixture into plastic or glass containers. Pour a thin layer of olive oil over the pesto to prevent discoloration, then seal.

Hot tomato and coriander sauce

4 large tomatoes, weighing approximately
    1 lb (450 g)
8 tbsp (120 g) fresh coriander leaves
    (cilantro)
2 small hot chilli peppers, fresh or canned
2 large onions, weighing approximately
    8 oz (225 g)
2 tbsp (30 ml) garlic vinegar

Put all the ingredients into a food processor and process finely for a few seconds. Alternatively, you can mince all the ingredients well and combine them in a bowl. Taste and add salt if required. Allow to cool, then pour into clean bottles, and label. This sauce is delicious served chilled with vegetable or meat dishes.

Tomato sauce with olives and oregano

1 lb (450 g) peeled tomatoes
3 tbsp (45 g) green pepper, chopped
1/2 large onion
1–2 cloves garlic
3 tbsp (45 ml) olive oil
10 green olives, stoned and chopped finely
1 tbsp (15 g) fresh oregano, chopped

Chop the onion and garlic finely and cook in the olive oil until softened and transparent. Add all the other ingredients, seasoning with salt and black pepper to taste. If you would like a smoother sauce you can combine all the ingredients in a blender or food processor and then return to the pan. Simmer gently for 5–10 minutes. Allow to cool, then pour into bottles, seal and label them. This sauce is ideal with cheese dishes, pasta or pork.

Elderflowers and elderberries both make delicious wines. Elderflower champagne is one of the most delicious drinks and it has the added bonus of being inexpensive and easy to make.

Alcoholic herbal sauce

1 pint (600 ml) vegetable or chicken stock
8 fl oz (225 ml) white wine, preferably
* medium-sweet German*
1 tbsp (15 g) fresh rosemary
1 tbsp (15 g) fresh dill
½ tbsp (7 g) fresh tarragon
3 tbsp (45 g) butter
3 tbsp (45 g) flour
½ tbsp (7 g) lemon peel, finely chopped

Mix the stock, wine and herbs together and simmer until reduced by 10–20 per cent. Melt the butter in a pan and add the flour, stirring vigorously, then cook for 5–10 minutes. Add the stock and wine mixture to the fat and flour by whisking it in with a small balloon whisk. Add the lemon peel and some salt and pepper to taste. Simmer for another 10 minutes. Strain the sauce to remove the herbs, allow to cool, then pour into bottles, seal and label. This sauce is delicious served hot with vegetables or poultry.

Mango and coriander sauce

1 medium mango
4 spring onions (shallots)
1 tbsp (15 g) grated fresh ginger root
½ tsp (2 g) garam masala
2 tbsp (30 ml) lime juice
1 tbsp (15 g) fresh coriander leaves
* (cilantro)*
1 tbsp (15 ml) sunflower or grapeseed oil

Heat the oil and gently cook the chopped spring onions (shallots) and ginger for about 5 minutes. Add the garam masala and cook for another couple of minutes.
  Chop the mango flesh finely, then add it and all the remaining ingredients to the pan. Stir well, then chill overnight in a

covered container in the fridge. The sauce can then be served as it is or processed in a blender to make it a little smoother. Allow to cool, then pour into bottles, seal and label them. This sauce is delicious with cold seafood, fish or chicken.

Coriander barbecue sauce

12 oz (350 g) finely chopped onions
4 garlic cloves, minced
4 oz (100 g) butter
12 fl oz (350 ml) tomato ketchup
¼ pint (150 ml) cheap brandy or sherry
2 tbsp (30 g) brown sugar
¼ tsp (1.2 g) cayenne pepper
2 tbsp (30 ml) lemon juice
¼ pint (150 ml) cider vinegar
1 tbsp (15 ml) Worcestershire sauce
4 fl oz (100 ml) water
1 tbsp (15 g) fresh coriander leaves

Soften the onions and garlic in the butter but do not let them brown. Add all the remaining ingredients and bring to the boil, stirring well. Simmer for 45 minutes, stirring occasionally. Allow to cool for a short while and then pour into jars. Cover tightly and label.

Spicy prunes with bergamot

1 lb (450 g) prunes
cold Indian tea
¾ pint (450 ml) cider vinegar
8 oz (225 g) demerara sugar
1 cinnamon stick
allspice berries
piece of ginger
6 cloves
5 bergamot leaves

Soak the prunes overnight in the cold tea. Place all the spices in a muslin bag and put

in a pan with the vinegar and sugar, heat until boiling and then cool. Cook the prunes in a little tea until they are soft, then drain and reserve the juice. Measure off ½ pint (300 ml) of the prune and tea liquor and mix with the spiced vinegar. Pour this liquid over the prunes, put into jars and cover. They will be ready within a week.

Packaging your goodies

When making mustards, savoury sauces and pickles, you can cover the lids in the same way as for sweet jams and jellies, but it can also look attractive to use hessian or calico. Plain calico is very inexpensive and could be stencilled to decorate the tops of sauces or pickles.

Packing a whole meal is an unusual idea — with the barbecue sauces you could package a bottle of the sauce with a pair of oven mitts, a packet of dried herbs to throw on to the barbecue and a pair of tongs. Gift-wrap all these together and you have something different for Father's Day! The pickles could be given with a decorated ham (see page 61) or just included in a hamper presentation.

HERBAL OILS AND VINEGARS

If you use tall elegant bottles or attractive old thick glass ones, a gift of oils and vinegars can look beautiful. As more and more recipes appear for salad dressings, so different flavoured oils and vinegars become more popular.

Mint and cranberry vinegar

1½ lb (675 g) fresh or frozen cranberries
2½ pints (1.5 l) red wine vinegar
12–14 fresh mint leaves

Save about a dozen of the best berries and put to one side. Chop the remaining fruit and place in a bowl. Boil the vinegar and pour over the berries. Cover and leave to infuse for 24 hours. Strain the vinegar through a kitchen sieve lined with muslin and press all the juice from the cranberries. Bring the juice to the boil and then allow to cool slightly. Pour into warm, clean bottles. Thread the reserved berries on to small bamboo skewers or satay sticks, with some mint leaves skewered in between them. Place a skewer in each bottle and seal with a lid or press in a cork. The vinegar will keep for about four months.

Parsley and lemon oil

1 pint (600 ml) virgin olive oil
1 small lemon, scrubbed
3 large sprigs parsley

Cut the lemon into quarters and slide the pieces on to a bamboo skewer or satay stick. Place in a jar, add the parsley and cover with oil. Leave to infuse for between one and two weeks in a warm place, shaking the jar daily.

Herb garden vinegar

2 pints (1.2 l) white wine vinegar
6 sprays each of thyme, rosemary, mint and
   summer savoury
4 large sprigs parsley
a good handful of tarragon
2 tbsp (30 g) coriander seeds
6 sticks celery, chopped
1 large onion, peeled and chopped
12 crushed green or black peppercorns

Place all the ingredients in a large jar or
bowl, cover, and leave for two to three
weeks in a warm place. Stir or shake from
time to time. Then strain off the vinegar
and bottle.

Old-fashioned herb sauce

1 stick horseradish, washed and scraped
2 small onions, peeled and chopped
4 sprigs each of winter savoury, basil,
   marjoram, thyme and tarragon
6 cloves
rind and juice of 1 lemon
½ pint (300 ml) red wine vinegar
1 pint (600 ml) water

Remove all the stalks from the herbs. Put
all the ingredients in a pan and simmer
gently for approximately 20 minutes. Then
strain and when cool pour into small
bottles. Cork securely. This sauce is useful
for flavouring stews and heavier dishes.

Rose petal vinegar

Fill a jar with the petals from a dark red or
pink scented rose bush. Press down well
and cover with white wine vinegar. Leave
in a moderately warm place for a month,
then strain and bottle.

Raspberry vinegar

*This very popular vinegar is very simple to make
and features in many current recipes. It is
delicious in salad dressings or even in fruit
salads.*

3 lb (1.3 kg) raspberries
3 pints (1.8 l) white wine vinegar
sugar

Put the raspberries and vinegar in a large
jar or bowl. Leave to infuse for ten days,
stirring daily. Strain off the vinegar and
add 2 oz (50 g) of sugar to each pint (600
ml) of vinegar. Place in a saucepan and
boil well. When cool, bottle and seal.

Olive oil with oregano

1 pint (600 ml) olive oil
5 sprigs fresh oregano
2 garlic cloves, peeled
8 whole green peppercorns
2 bay leaves

Either pour the oil into a jar with a tightly
fitting cork lid or leave it in its bottle and
add the herbs. It will take several days for
the herby flavour to develop. The oil can
then be left as it is or strained and poured
back into the container, with a fresh piece
of oregano, in order to identify the oil.
   The same process can be used for most
herbs, but particularly successful oils are
made from basil, fennel, rosemary, marjoram, thyme, tarragon and dill.

DRINKS AND SYRUPS

In this section I have given two of my
favourite recipes. The elderflower champagne definitely rates far higher than any

French creations, and the rosehip syrup is delicious on ice cream or as a base for fruit salads.

Elderflower champagne

8 pints (4.8 l) water
1 large lemon, scrubbed
5 elderflower heads
1½ lb (675 g) granulated sugar
2 tsp (10 ml) white vinegar

Heat a little of the water and dissolve the sugar in it, then allow to cool. Squeeze the lemon, then place the juice and the skins with the elderflowers in an immaculately clean bucket. Add the vinegar and the rest of the cold water. Leave for about four to five days, then strain and pour into sterilized bottles. It is important that the bottles are screw-topped, not corked. (Corks might pop out of the bottles during fermentation.) The champagne will be ready to drink after a week and does not improve with lengthy keeping.

Rosehip syrup

2 lb (900 g) rosehips, finely chopped
5 pints (3 l) water
1 lb (450 g) granulated sugar

Place 3½ pints (2.1 l) of water in a large saucepan and add the rosehips. Bring to the boil then remove from the heat and leave for 15 minutes. Ladle the mixture into a jelly bag or double thickness of muslin and leave to drain for several hours. Return the pulp to the saucepan with the remaining water and boil. Leave as before and then strain through the jelly bag or muslin. Pour the liquor into a saucepan and simmer until it reduces to approximately 1½–2 pints (900 ml–1.2 l) and add the sugar. Stir until the sugar has dissolved and then boil for five minutes. Allow to cool a little and then pour into clean, warm bottles and cork securely.

Packaging the presents

Both these ideas can be packaged attractively with some custom-made labels. You could stencil a design on to the label if you don't trust your freehand drawing, or you could just rely on neat lettering. The elderflower champagne could be packaged with a pretty set of glasses or perhaps a good book — my idea of heaven is a glass of chilled elderflower champagne and a fascinating book! The rosehip syrup could be part of a rose-themed basket of goodies, containing rose petal jelly, rose vinegar, damson and rose jam and a couple of beautiful pink roses for the finishing touch.

HERBAL CHEESES

A collection of herbal cheeses, with some home-made breads and biscuits, would be well received by many friends or relatives and they are easily made and not overly expensive. They are best when freshly made, rather than frozen, and if they are rushed off to the recipient they might even arrive still warm! If you do have to freeze these recipes you should cover them well with foil and label them. Allow them to thaw for at least two or three hours at room temperature, depending on the size of container used.

Making your own cheese is a fairly lengthy process, so I would suggest you cheat and use bought cheeses as your base.

Soft cheese with herbs

4 oz (100 g) soft full-fat or half-fat cheese
2 oz (50 g) butter
1½ tbsp (22 g) finely chopped parsley
1 tbsp (15 g) mixed fresh herbs including
* marjoram, thyme and dill*
½ tsp (2.5 g) freshly ground black pepper

Mix all the ingredients in a food processor, then turn out into a small bowl and keep in the fridge. This cheese can either be served in a small pot or ramekin, or moulded into a shape and wrapped in a large leaf.

Curd cheese with mint and orange

8 oz (225 g) curd cheese
zest of 1 orange
1 tsp (5 g) finely chopped fresh mint
curls of orange peel
small mint leaves

Mix all the ingredients thoroughly and turn into small ramekin dishes. Smooth the tops and decorate each one with a curl of orange peel and a small mint leaf.

Cream cheese with basil and garlic

8 oz (225 g) cream cheese
1 tbsp (15 g) finely chopped sweet basil
1 clove garlic, minced

Mix all the ingredients well and pack into small containers. This cheese is excellent stuffed in small tomatoes and eaten with warm French bread.

Herby cheese marbles

8 oz (225 g) full-fat cream cheese
various herbs and spices, including chives,
* dill, parsley, mint, poppy seeds, sesame*
* seeds, caraway seeds and oregano*

Make sure the herbs are very finely chopped, then place in separate plates. Roll small amounts of the cream cheese into balls and then roll in one of the herbs or spices to give an even coating. Choose a reasonable variety of herbs and spices as this adds to the visual effect. Pile on to a flat dish or wooden platter and decorate with a bundle of fresh herbs.

Presenting your cheeses

All these cheeses look attractive in small white or terracotta pots. You could also wrap the pots in a large circle of gingham or spotted cotton. Several pots wrapped in co-ordinating or matching cotton bundles with a bundle of fresh herbs and a fresh loaf of garlic or herby bread would be very welcome indeed.

HERBAL BREADS

Bread is delicious when given the careful addition of a few herbs. Garlic bread is well-known and well-loved, but these breads are a little bit different. They will prove equally popular with your family and friends.

Mixed fresh herb bread

1 French loaf
½ tsp (2.5 g) salt and pepper
3 oz (75 g) butter
2 tbsp (30 g) fresh mixed herbs, finely
  chopped

Mix the herbs, salt and pepper with the butter until it is smooth. Make diagonal cuts roughly every inch (2.5 cm) along the loaf, cutting deep but not completely through the loaf. Spread the herb butter on each slice until you have used it all up. Wrap well in foil and store the loaf in the fridge until needed. To serve, heat it in a hot oven at 400°F (200°C), Gas Mark 6, for 5–10 minutes.

Other possible combinations for herb breads include lemon, parsley and dill (add the zest and juice of half a lemon and change the herbs); rosemary, chervil and orange (add the zest and juice of half an orange and change the herbs).

Strawberry and mint soda bread

8 oz (225 g) wholemeal flour
8 oz (225 g) plain flour
½ tsp (2.5 g) salt
1 tsp (5 g) bicarbonate of soda
2 oz (50 g) butter
6 oz (175 ml) carton strawberry yoghurt
¼ pint (150 ml) milk
2 tbsp (30 g) finely chopped fresh mint

Sift the flours, salt and soda into a bowl and rub in the butter until the mixture resembles fine breadcrumbs. Add the yoghurt, mint and enough milk to make a fairly stiff dough. Shape the dough into a ball, place on a greased baking sheet, flatten it slightly and score with a sharp knife. Sprinkle with flour and bake in a moderately hot oven — 400°F (200°C) or Gas Mark 6 — for 30 minutes. Leave to cool on a cake rack.

Cheese and herb scones

These are delicious eaten with soup or cheese and are made very quickly.

1½ oz (40 g) butter
8 oz (225 g) plain flour
2 tsp (10 g) baking powder
½ tsp (2.5 g) salt
¼ tsp (1 g) cayenne pepper
3 oz (75 g) hard cheese, grated
¼ pint (150 ml) milk
1 tbsp (15 g) fresh herbs, finely chopped

Sift the baking powder, cayenne pepper, salt and flour into a bowl. Chop the butter and mix with the flour until it resembles breadcrumbs. Add the cheese, milk and herbs and stir with a knife to form a soft dough.

Form a ball and divide into eight pieces. Pat each piece into a circle ½ in (12 mm) thick. Place the scones on a greased baking sheet with plenty of space between them. Bake for 10–15 minutes in a very hot oven — 450°F (230°C) or Gas Mark 8 — until they are risen and golden. Either serve immediately or cool on a wire rack. These are best eaten as soon as possible (this is never a problem!)

HERBS AROUND THE HOUSE

Although dried herbs are usually thought of in a culinary context, they are also very attractive in their own right and make beautiful flower arrangements and decorations. There is the added bonus that they smell wonderful and the fragrance will gently perfume the air around them. There are many ways to use dried flowers and herbs, and this chapter contains some suggestions and ideas to inspire you. The majority of herbs used in this chapter have been air-dried, although a small number have been glycerined or preserved in silica gel.

HERBS GARLANDS AND WREATHS

Garlands and wreaths give a lovely welcome to your friends and guests: hang one on the front door or, if the weather is too damp, just inside the hallway. Although many of us associate garlands with festive occasions, they look equally beautiful at any time of year, and with a dried herb garland you have the added bonus of the subtle aroma that pervades the room. They also make excellent presents for friends or your hostess, because they show that a little extra thought and time has been put into the gift.

You can buy twig wreaths or ones made from natural grapevines and hops as bases to work on, and then add the chosen herbs. The easiest method of attaching dried items to a wreath base is by using a hot glue gun. I am a very keen proponent of the glue gun when it is used in a careful professional manner (large amounts of unnecessary glue all over the article look dreadful). The guns themselves are fairly reasonable in price and have myriad uses, so are a worthwhile investment for any keen dried flower enthusiast. They are easily bought from hardware stores and other household shops. Alternatively, the flowers can be wired on to the wreath base, which is the traditional method. It works well, but its main drawback is the amount of time it takes. Also, a badly

All these arrangements include herbs. The large basket with peonies has some lovely soft green oregano in it and others contain Alchemilla, *marjoram, lavender and sage.*

wired wreath can be a mass of wires and look unsightly.

There are many varieties of herbs being dried commercially for decorative use. Although they are more expensive to buy than to grow, you may prefer to buy them if you are using large quantities for an arrangement. The main range of herbs being dried successfully on a commercial scale include those listed below.

Pot marjoram A lovely dark lilac/mauve cluster which looks particularly stunning with bright red 'Mercedes' roses.

Oregano The knotted oregano or marjoram is a subtle shade of greeny-grey and makes a wonderful filler.

Dill/fennel This yellow umbrel of flowers makes a dainty addition to any arrangement and when well dried is very effective. Cow parsley looks very similar but is white.

Agastache This is a minty-smelling plant with a strong spear or plume of blue/grey or green flowers. It not only makes a strong base for an arrangement but also smells fantastic!

Bay leaves These are available in sprays or as individual leaves which can be wired for arrangements. Their strong green colour makes them good fillers.

Lavender This perennial favourite is available in various types but the bigger flowered variety from Provence makes the best splash of colour in a display. If you wire a small clump of stems together the effect is much improved.

Hops These are very popular for sleep-inducing pillows, but also make wonderfully decorative dried plants. Entire hop bines look very dramatic wound round pillars or doorways as a centrepiece to a dried display. A hop bine attached along the length of a beam in an old property looks pretty and gives a very countrified atmosphere.

Other herbs

There are many other herbs that lend themselves to decorative use but are not so widely available commercially. However, if you grow and dry them yourself you can increase the range you have to work with. Other varieties that are worth trying include the following herbs.

Mints All of them are suitable when in flower and should be air-dried.

Rosemary Air-drying is adequate but makes the sprigs rather brittle. An unusual effect can be obtained by glycerining rosemary — it goes a gun-metal grey and looks very pretty.

Thyme All the species can be air-dried but they are very small and so are best used in smaller displays or in wreaths and garlands.

Sage All the varieties air-dry to a good colour. They look slightly withered but make good scented fillers.

Using herbs and flowers

Many of the herbal flowers can be preserved in silica gel but they should then be used in small-scale work. Dainty circles of borage flowers intertwined with small sprays of thyme, parsley (also dried in silica gel), comfrey and chive flowers look enchanting.

Dried herbs blend well with other dried flowers, and obviously dried roses and peonies span the divide well. Peonies were at one time thought to be divine plants that would ward off evil spirits, and to some extent one must agree — they are truly divine, in my opinion, and among the most beautiful plants in the garden. Whether they will guard against evil spirits you must decide for yourself! Roses look beautiful whether they are fresh, dried, whole, buds or in separate petals. They are such useful plants and, with that combination of virtues, deserve to be grown in everyone's gardens.

Allium heads might also be called herbal decorations, but I would particularly recommend the flower of the common leek as it has a pink tinge and is smaller and more manageable than some of the huge decorative forms of allium. There are several grey foliages that dry well from the herb garden, including *Santolina* and *Artemisia*. The overall colour or feel that comes from dried herbs is a misty heathery grey/lavender effect which is subtle and beautiful if used delicately.

A hot glue gun can be invaluable when working with dried flowers. Whether you are edging a basket or making up a wreath, the glue gun will fix the flowers firmly and quickly.

Using herbs and spices

Dried flowers and herbs need not just be used to fill baskets and other containers — they can also be attached to the outside rim of the basket. An edging of roses and marjoram looks stunning and the basket can then be used for pot-pourri or just filled with a few pine cones. A culinary arrangement for the kitchen could incorporate some cloves of garlic and bundles of spices. Cinnamon sticks always look attractive and give a little fragrance to an arrangement. If the scent seems to be fading, it can be revived by dropping a little cinnamon essential oil on to the sticks themselves.

Many spices look pretty when incorporated into a dried display. Root ginger takes on an almost coral-like effect when it is peeled and dried. Star anise has a strong aniseed smell and is a pretty star-shaped accent for any small-scale work. Nutmegs in their natural state are useful all year round, but look lovely in Christmas arrangements and wreaths when sprayed gold or silver.

Making herbal posies

Small posies can be made from herbs and spices to give as hostess gifts or to lay beside each place setting for a dinner party. These little spice posies are very popular in Germany, Scandinavia and several other parts of Europe. The posies are a traditional gift and sometimes include pearls, beads and flowers made from sunflower seeds and other tiny treasures.

The individual ingredients are placed on a wire. This is done either by passing the wire around the spice or sprig of herbs, or by using a hot glue gun to attach the wire. The wire can be hidden by judicious use of a gold coiled wire called bouillon, which is wrapped around the wired spice to camouflage the wire.

The various items are then assembled. Choose a small rose or other suitable centrepiece for the middle of the posy and then arrange several other items in a circle around the rose and wire them tightly together. Further concentric circles are then added until you reach the size of posy you require. To finish the posy professionally, you can buy a stiffened cotton posy frill which can be attached, and the stems neatened at the same time, by binding the wires together with florists' tape. You can hide any other mechanics that remain visible with plenty of ribbon. Other ingredients can include nuts, pine cones, beads and pearls, all of which are available from floral suppliers (see stockists on page 126).

DRIED HERB POSIES AND BOUQUETS

Larger bouquets can be made in the same way to achieve a traditional Victorian-style posy which looks extremely pretty on a dressing table or when placed on a hall or side table. A modern alternative to wiring posies the traditional way is to use a handle with some florists' foam on the end, into which the flowers and herbs are pushed. This takes away the need for wiring and gives an equally pretty finished effect.

There are several herb-related flowers that would look particularly suitable in an old-fashioned posy, with clove pinks and carnations being two of the most obvious examples. It would be fun to refer to the

secret language of flowers and send a subtle message with your present: rosemary for remembrance, zinnia for absent friends, basil for good wishes or mint for virtue.

Simple tied bunches can also look very effective, with a selection of herbs and foliages all tied together with a generous bow.

COUNTRY-STYLE HATS

Country-style straw hats can be decorated with the products of the herb garden and then given to an enthusiastic gardener to keep off the sun while he or she is working in the garden. Having said that, many people would feel that a straw hat, prettily decorated with dried flowers and herbs, is far too precious to be worn! So perhaps it would be better to suggest hanging it on the wall for display.

You can use any large straw hat or boater. Hats made from natural materials look far more suitable for the dried flower treatment than those made from man-made materials. Tie a pretty ribbon, in the colour on which your colour scheme is based, around the crown of the hat and finish with a large bow with streamers. A ribbon can be made from the printed cotton material of your choice. Cut it to the length you need but double the width and then machine it, right sides together, before turning it inside out. It is quicker to finish the ends by hand.

Once the ribbon is in place you can choose a selection of dried herbs and flowers to tone with the ribbon and the hat. Several larger flowers make a good central point but you will need some soft feathery pieces to soften the arrangement. Although it is perfectly possible to wire

ingredients on to the brim, the finished effect is usually a little untidy. Instead, use a hot glue gun.

Presentation ideas
A decorated hat can give a country feel to a bedroom or kitchen and would make a lovely present. If it is for a keen gardener, you could pack it with an old-fashioned garden trug for collecting cut flowers and a pair of good secateurs. The image conjured up by these props is one of drifting through an English garden on a warm day, gently cutting one scented rose after another before wandering back to the house to arrange them and wait for tea. An impossible dream, maybe, but one that's fun to imagine!

HERBS WITH CHINA AND GLASS

Although natural and rustic accessories relate better to dried flowers and herbs in general, sometimes porcelain and glass can work just as well. Blue and white Delft china can look quite stunning with a peach and blue arrangement containing 'Gerda' roses, *Eryngium* (sea holly), blue *Agastache* and lavender, with white dill or cow parsley as a highlight.

Glass can work well with dried flowers if it is filled with pot-pourri or small pine cones to disguise the stems or florists' foam. A square glass tank filled with foam and then small cones would look wonderful with a mass of dried 'Tamara' roses (a lovely porcelain pink), glycerined beech, fennel seed heads, oregano and marjoram. You can always increase the intensity of the fragrance by adding fennel or marjoram essential oils to the cones.

HERBS AT CHRISTMAS

Festive arrangements with dried and pre-served materials always look especially lovely at Christmas and other holiday times. We all make more effort for special occasions and want our houses to look particularly warm and welcoming. As there are many presents given and parties to go to during this festive season, this is a good opportunity to give something just a little out of the ordinary.

Dried herbs blend in very well with more traditional Christmas decorations such as pine cones, nuts and cinnamon sticks. Gilded poppy heads mixed with bunches of roses, purple marjoram, gilded cones and dark burgundy tartan ribbons look amazing. In many cases, reasonably-sized clusters of a herb look much more powerful than individual sprays, which give a much weaker effect.

(Previous page)
Garlic has been fixed on a spiral around the basket to add to the gourmet feel of this display. Many herbs have been used in the arrangement to ensure it smells as good as it looks.

The summery straw hat has been decorated with glycerined rosemary, delphiniums, Agastache and lavender to give a misty blue combination.

A *cautionary note*

Ivory or natural beeswax candles blend in with most colour schemes and give an elegant, traditional feel to an arrangement. Welcoming flowers and scents are a sure way to make guests feel at home and comfortable. One note of caution, how-ever: by their very nature, dried materials are a fire hazard, and if you are arranging them with candles that will be lit, they must not be left unattended. Make sure the candles are well above the arrangement and blow them out and replace them once they burn down too near the foliage. Dried flower arrangements must also not be placed too near open fires where sparks can set light to them. Apart from this problem with fire, the only other hazard seems to be cats, who love dried flowers and foliage at the best of times. Include plenty of dried herbs, especially catmint, in an arrangement and you can probably guarantee a good cabaret while the cat races around ripping the arrangement to pieces!

HERBS ON THE CHRISTMAS TREE

There are several spots on the Christmas tree where you could tuck a herbal arrangement or tiny wreaths of herbal flowers and foliage to add to the natural pine scent of the tree. Decorated pine cones with clusters of herbs and ribbons to hang on the tree, and miniature baskets of dried herbs tied with a festive gold cord, add an unusual touch and fragrance. As there are so many family gatherings at this time of year, why not make some decorations for the tree as a family present?

Miniature sacks

A miniature sack of herbs can be made from a piece of hessian 6 × 2 in (15 x 5 cm). fold it in half along the longer edge and stitch together the two side seams. Turn it right sides out, fill with strong-smelling dried herbs and tie with an elastic band. Then decorate the sack with a red or green ribbon, miniature pine cones and some holly.

Stockings filled with herbs

Small socks or stockings can be cut from any cotton material with a festive colour scheme or pattern. Cut out two identical pieces and sew round the edges, leaving the top open. If you sew with a contrasting thread, say holly green on red material, it doesn't matter if the stitches show as they can be part of the design. Alternatively, you can place the two pieces of material with right sides together and sew with a matching cotton, then very carefully turn the stocking inside out. This is more fiddly but looks neater. Then fill the stocking with scented dried herbs and stitch across the top. The stocking can then be decorated with festive bits and pieces, such as gold-sprayed miniature cones and holly berries.

Little balls of herbs

Small polystyrene spheres, 1 in (2.5 cm) in diameter, can be made into herbal Christmas tree decorations. Cover them in a solution of latex adhesive, watered down slightly so it is easier to apply. Dip these balls in dried lavender or stick herbal flower heads, such as oregano or marjoram, all over the balls and trim with tiny ribbons. A set of balls in shades of misty lavender and greeny-grey, trimmed with narrow pale pink ribbons, looks very dainty and unusual.

CHRISTMAS SWAGS AND GARLANDS

A swag of dried herbs and flowers hung across a mantelpiece or round a doorway is a lovely way of welcoming your guests. If you have the time and patience, you could make one for a friend and give it as a wonderful pre-Christmas surprise. Placing unusual herbal foliage or flowers in a festive garland provides extra points of interest. Cones and berries are a must for a traditional look, whether left in their natural shades or gilded. Small kumquats could be included because they are daintier than oranges. Tartan ribbons and bunches of lavender, bay, holly, rosemary and sage are complemented by sprays of brilliant red roses, cream peonies and pink carnations. Dried flowers can look just as lovely as fresh arrangements and last far longer.

However, another warning note must be sounded regarding mantelpiece arrangements. Do take care to fix the swag very firmly across the mantelpiece, as open fires and dried flowers do not mix and it only takes seconds for an arrangement to fall into the dying embers of a fire and go up in smoke.

*This pretty collection of sacks and
stockings smells delicious. You could
also make lavender and cinnamon
bundles to decorate the Christmas tree
or to attach to parcels.*

Making a swag or garland

Although somewhat time-consuming, swags or garlands are not too difficult to make. Measure the length of decoration required and cut a piece of rope or coloured cord to that measurement, plus 4 in (10 cm) for loops at each end. Choose your combination of ingredients (you will need more than you think), including some ribbons, something bulky like pine cones and a selection of foliage such as spruce or holly to form the basis of the swag.

Wire all the ingredients into small bunches approximately 3 in (7.5 cm) long using fine floristry wire. Make plenty of bunches of each type of ingredient. Pine cones are wired by inserting the end of a medium strength wire into the scales and then wrapping it around the cone, leaving a stem to wire on to the garland.

Taking the piece of cord, bend 2 in (5 cm) over at each end and wire on to the main cord to make a strong loop. Start with a feathery piece of foliage and, using a fine to medium strength piece of wire, attach it to the cord. Trim off the excess wire once the bunch is attached. Continue along the cord wiring with a new piece of wire for each bunch and trimming any unnecessary wire each time. When you reach the middle of the length of cord, turn the bunches so that they face the opposite direction. You may have to wire extra very short bunches into the middle to pad it out a little, or alternatively you can get out that glue gun again!

BEAUTIFUL HERBS

The luxury of home-made herbal beauty products is something no one can resist. The subtle and evocative smell of rosemary in the bathwater or a cooling application of chilled lavender water is a sensuous luxury. Unlike most luxuries, though, the cost of these ones need not be tremendous. Once you have collected some basic ingredients all you need is a little experimentation and a keen eye for unusual containers, and you are ready to begin.

BASIC INGREDIENTS

The most important consideration to bear in mind when making herbal preparations is to only use the best quality products you can find. Good quality oils and natural essential oils will combine to make a far superior product than that produced by cheap oil and chemical, synthetic oils. Natural products are far less likely to cause skin allergies, but it is always wise to test your finished product on a small patch of your own skin if not on that of the recipient.

Essential oils are produced from many different scented plants, using both the leaf and stalk, or flower, depending on the plant concerned. Although it is possible to extract these essential oils yourself, it is a long process and the fun of making some herbal beauty products as gifts is to have fairly instant results. If you find concocting potions really appealing there are plenty of opportunities for further experimentation to be found in the many specialist books available.

PACKAGING

As with every product, it is the packaging that gives the finishing touch and makes all the difference between something that

Soaps, pot-pourri and other scented gifts are always popular, and particularly so if you have made them yourself.

looks home-made and slightly dubious or exciting and luxurious. If you keep your eyes open in antique shops and jumble sales you will discover that there are plenty of old and interesting bottles around. Thick glass bottles in a green or blue tone can look wonderful when decorated with a pretty satin ribbon and a few flowers. Sealing is probably best done with a cork, which can be trimmed to fit any size of bottle. Screw-top bottles are another possibility but they don't have the same old-fashioned appeal.

Another lovely idea is to buy a glass scent bottle with a ground stopper to prevent evaporation. The container could then be treasured and reused many times. Atomisers can give a marvellous feeling of luxury to some home-made scented waters. As shown in the photograph, there are many unusual perfume bottles available and they make a stunning display on a pretty dressing table. As a complete contrast, there are also some promisingly shaped containers to be found in grocery stores and supermarkets: if you look carefully next time you are shopping you'll be amazed at how many suitable shapes and sizes there are amongst the mustard pots, vinegar jars, mayonnaise jars or even bottles of squashes and cordials. You may have to cover the lid, or substitute a cork for the screw top depending on how attractive it is once opened, but nevertheless there is plenty of scope.

Always label your product carefully and add instructions if it should be kept in the refrigerator or in cool conditions. Giving a use-by date might also be a good idea if something has a fairly short life. Labels can be decorated by hand or stencilled and

tied with a ribbon around the neck of the bottle. You could also use a sticky label and attach it to the body of the bottle. Several products can then be packaged together in a hamper or basket, with cotton wool balls or other packaging to fill the basket and prevent the bottles breaking. Home-made pot-pourri makes a very good filler for baskets — you can carefully arrange a selection of bottles amongst the pot-pourri, then cover the basket with swathes of cellophane before decorating it with a pretty bow.

BATH-TIME PRODUCTS

Nothing works more magic than a per-fumed soak in a warm bath after a really tiring or stressful day. The smell of the herbal products can add a great deal to that relaxation and many bath preparations are very simple to make.

There are two main groups of herbs in these preparations: herbs to promote re-laxation and those that help to revive you. The relaxing herbs include camomile, scented geranium, jasmine, lavender, neroli (orange blossom) and hops. The more stimulating and reviving herbs include basil, lemon verbena, rosemary, melissa and bergamot.

Although it is a tempting thought to strew freshly picked herbs across the waters of your calming bath, I wouldn't recommend that you try it! Speaking from bitter experience, it causes untold blockage problems in the plumbing and feels very uncomfortable when you sit on a particu-larly sharp stalk! The best way to use fresh herbs is to place them in a muslin bath bag.

Bath bags

Cut out some 9-in (22.5-cm) diameter circles of muslin and place 2 tablespoons (30 g) of roughly torn fresh herbs in the middle of each one. Dried herbs are just as successful. Gather the edges of the circle together and make into a small bundle, holding it in place with an elastic band. Then attach ribbons around the bundle to cover the elastic band, making a long enough loop to hang it from the taps so it will dangle in the water. A set of bath bags, with different coloured ribbons to denote different herbs or mixtures of herbs, could be put together with a collection of other bath-time treats. Do write clear instructions on a label so they don't get mistaken for bouquet garni and put in a stew!

Oatmeal can be added to the contents of the bath bags — use equal quantities of herbs and oatmeal — as it helps to soften the skin.

Bath oils

These are very simple to make and very relaxing. The oil base should be good quality — preferably almond for normal to dry skin or safflower for normal to greasy skin. The only oil that will completely disperse in bathwater is a form of castor oil called turkey red oil. However, it is not easily available in health food stores, unlike the others, and so I would recom-mend trying the almond or safflower oils instead.

Choose some essential oils that will relax or revive (see the suggestions above) and make sure they are good quality natural oils rather than chemical ones. Chemical fragrances are excellent for pot-pourris and products that will not come into contact with the skin, but it is safer to

(Opposite)
Bath bags are simple to assemble and make a very relaxing bath that smells wonderful. They are a refreshing change from a gift of bath salts.

(Above)
There are many scent bottles available that would make lovely containers for your herbal bath potions and gifts. Alternatively you can collect old bottles that appeal to you, perhaps because of their unusual colour or shape.

use natural oils for skin preparations, in case the recipient is allergic to the chemical ones.

To make the oils, add 5 drops of essential oil to every tablespoon (15 ml) of almond or safflower oil that you put into the bottle. Shake well before use. You can use just one essential oil, such as rosemary or lavender, or you can mix them — rose and lavender, or rosemary and orange are good blends. The possibilities are endless and the fun starts when you begin to choose your essential oils. These should be available at your local health food store or beauty shop.

WASHBALLS AND SOAPS

Washballs date back to Elizabethan times and so are traditional shapes of soap. Making soap at home can be rather time-consuming, so I have included a recipe that uses a pure, fragrance-free ready-made soap to speed up the process. Traditionally, soap is made with tallow, which is rendered or melted animal fat. It should be available from your local butcher and you can melt it in a heavy saucepan over a low heat and then strain it into screw-top jam jars for storage. Take care when making soap as the caustic soda that is used can burn your skin, so do wear rubber gloves and handle it with care.

Lavender and rose washballs

2 × 5 oz (150 g) bars plain Castille soap, finely grated
8 fl oz (225 ml) rose or lavender water
5 drops lavender essential oil
5 drops rose essential oil

Heat 3 fl oz (75 ml) of the rose or lavender water and pour it over the soap. Let it stand for about ten minutes. Mix well and then incorporate the rose and lavender oils. Leave to harden for two days. Then make the mixture into small balls, each one about the size of a table tennis ball or slightly smaller, and leave to dry in a dry airy place. When the washballs have completely hardened you can polish them with a cloth moistened with the rest of the rose or lavender water, or alternatively wet your hands with the rose or lavender water and rub the balls between your hands. Allow to dry out before packaging.

Floral vinegar for the bath

Floral vinegars can soften the skin when used in the bath and are very refreshing if kept in the fridge and dabbed on to a fevered brow in moments of stress! Cider vinegar has a delicate apple scent and so makes an excellent base.

There are several herbs and flowers that can be mixed with the vinegar. The main consideration will probably be which ingredients are easiest for you to obtain. Successful plants include jasmine flowers, rose petals, lavender flowers and stalks, scented geranium leaves, lemon balm or lemon verbena leaves and rosemary.

Place a large handful of mixed flowers and herbs or a single variety (rose and lavender with a little jasmine works well, or scented geranium and lemon verbena) in a glass bottle and fill up with cider vinegar. Replace the lid or seal with a cork and place in a sunny spot for a couple of weeks. Then strain the vinegar, making sure that you release as much moisture from the herbs as possible, and pour into a measuring jug. Half-fill a bottle with the scented vinegar and top up with spring water. One bottle of vinegar will therefore fill two bottles of the same size with the floral vinegar. To use, pour a generous quantity into the bath with the taps full on.

Orange blossom bath salts

8 oz (225 g) baking soda
1 lb (450 g) coarse sea salt
1/2 fl oz (12 ml) neroli (orange blossom) essential oil

Stir together the baking soda and sea salt, then add the essential oil and store in a

sealed jar. Food colouring may be added if you wish. Use three tablespoons (45 g) per bath.

Lemon verbena bubbles

12 oz (350 g) pure soap flakes
3/4 pint (450 ml) spring water
1/4 fl oz (6 ml) lemon verbena essential oil
1 fl oz (25 ml) vodka
2 fl oz (50 ml) glycerine

Heat the water and dissolve the soap flakes in it. In another container, mix the essential oil with the glycerine and vodka. Combine these two mixtures and add a drop of yellow or green food colouring if you wish. Store in a wide-mouthed jar with a sealed lid.

Orange and cinnamon soap

4 fl oz (100 ml) spring water
2 tbsp (30 g) caustic soda
4 oz (100 g) melted tallow
1 tsp (5 ml) neroli (orange blossom)
  essential oil
1 tsp (5 ml) cinnamon essential oil
4 fl oz (100 ml) safflower oil

Wearing rubber gloves, pour the water into a large heat-proof glass bowl. Add the caustic soda and stir well with a wooden spoon. Add the melted tallow and stir vigorously. Then add the safflower oil and the neroli and cinnamon essential oils. Beat well and pour into plastic moulds. Leave to set. Once they are set ease the soaps out of the moulds and leave in a dry airy place for two weeks.

Cucumber and mint soap

4 fl oz (100 ml) spring water
large bunch of fresh mint, any variety
2 tbsp (30 g) caustic soda
4 oz (100 g) white vegetable fat, melted
6 drops mint essential oil
8 fl oz (225 ml) almond oil
1/2 cucumber

Liquidize, or place in a food processor, the mint leaves and spring water. Pour into a bowl and leave for a couple of hours. Liquidize (or process) the cucumber. Strain the spring water into a large heat-proof glass bowl, discarding the mint leaves, then add the caustic soda (making sure you are wearing rubber gloves). Stir with a wooden spoon then add the melted vegetable fat. Add 4 tbsp (60 g) of cucumber purée, the almond oil and mint essential oil. Beat well and then pour the mixture into plastic moulds. Small soaps can be made in shaped ice cube moulds or larger ones in yoghurt pots or similar containers. Leave to set for two days.

Gently ease the soaps out of the moulds and then leave in an airing cupboard or other dry airy place for two weeks before using.

Note: It can help to line the moulds with cling film as this may overcome any problems in removing the soap once it has set.

HIDDEN HERBS

There are many uses for herbs in sachets, pot-pourri, pillows and other containers where the herbs may not be visible but release their delicious scents. No one could resist a lovely collection of lacy herb sachets for their cupboards or linens. Most of these ideas are very simple to make, yet are perfect presents for all generations. The sachets and pillows can be varied according to the likes and dislikes of the recipients. Many inexpensive fabrics can be used and then decorated, so none of these ideas need be expensive.

HERBAL POT-POURRI

Pot-pourri is a very traditional aromatic accessory for the home, and many recipes have been handed down through the generations. There are several ways to make pot-pourri. The oldest method is for a moist pot-pourri, where layers of rose petals, spices and salt are arranged in a large crock and left to rot down for six weeks or more. The strength of scent is excellent but the visual appearance is not good (the salt bleaches out all the colour in the rose petals). That is why traditional pot-pourri jars are closed, with holes for the fragrance to waft through.

A prettier finished effect is gained by mixing flowers and herbs with essential oils and a fixative, such as orris root. This is also a fairly lengthy method but the finished effect can be lovely, particularly if some flowers are dried with silica gel and placed on top for decoration.

As most of the projects in this chapter are for sachets or other items where the herbs are hidden away behind some fabric, the look of the finished pot-pourri is not of paramount importance. The main point is that the scent should be strong and long-lasting. When making small sachets it helps to use fairly small ingredients of an even size, so there are no unsightly lumps and bulges in the sachets. The best answer for this is to use small sprigs of dried herbs and flowers with a much larger proportion of fixative.

Many recipes call for powdered orris

Herbal pillows, sachets and cushions can come in all shapes and sizes. It's easy to slip a sachet of herbs into a cushion and then remove it for refilling when the smell starts to fade.

root, but I use cut and sifted orris or blue flag root instead, as I find the powder spoils the outward appearance of pot-pourri. However, as the recipes here are mainly for use in sachets, either powdered or cut orris root will do. (For stockists, see page 126.)

Many of the recipes here can easily be altered to suit whatever ingredients you have available. Once you have made several batches of your own pot-pourri you will become more courageous and want to experiment. It is easy to make up your own recipes — just keep to the basic guidelines on quantities of ingredients.

Orris root and oil mixture
As a general note, I use a measuring jug when measuring out the various dry ingredients, unless they are measured by the spoonful. The orris root is best mixed with the essential oil first and put into a small screw-top jar to mature for a couple of days. If you are intending to make several types of pot-pourri, I would suggest you build up a collection of jars with different orris root and essential oil mixtures which you can use as you wish.

Mix the oil and orris root in the proportions of 4 oz (100 g) orris root to ½ fl oz (12 ml) essential oil. Once it has matured for a couple of days you can use it by the tablespoonful (per 15 g) as indicated in the recipes. Make sure that you label the jars clearly, stating the particular essential oil you have used. The collection of orris root/oil jars can then sit in a neat row on your kitchen shelf or worktop, where you can shake them occasionally to encourage the mixing process. Avoid storing them in strong sunlight as it will reduce the strength of the essential oils.

Delicious mint and cinnamon pot-pourri

½ pint (300 ml) cinnamon pieces
½ pint (300 ml) mint leaves, crumbled
2 tbsp (30 g) cinnamon/orris mixture
1 tbsp (15 g) apple/orris mixture
½ tbsp (7 g) mint/orris mixture

Use a large mixing bowl and mix together all the ingredients. As these recipes are mainly destined for use in sachets, you should break the cinnamon pieces up fairly small. Having mixed it well, turn the mixture into a large jar or polythene bag and seal. Put it away for two to four weeks, shaking it regularly to ensure even distribution of the oil mixtures. Check the smell after two weeks: if the aroma seems satisfactory you can use it, but if not you should wait another couple of weeks. If you are still not happy with the smell, try adding other orris root/oil mixes until you like the balance of the fragrance.

Lemon pot-pourri

¼ pint (150 ml) lemon verbena leaves
¼ pint (150 ml) lemon balm leaves
¼ pint (150 ml) lemon thyme leaves
½ pint (300 ml) lemon and orange peel, dried and chopped
1 tbsp (15 g) bay leaves, crumbled
¼ pint (150 ml) mint leaves
3 tbsp (45 g) lemon/orris mixture
2 tbsp (30 g) neroli (orange blossom)/orris mixture
1 tbsp (75 g) mint/orris mixture

Mix all the ingredients together in a large mixing bowl and place in a large jar or polythene bag. Seal and put away in a dark place for two to four weeks, shaking occasionally to help the mixing process.

Herbs and spices pot-pourri

½ pint (300 ml) ginger root
¼ pint (150 ml) cinnamon sticks
¼ pint (150 ml) star anise
3–4 nutmegs, broken
¼ pint (150 ml) angelica root
6–8 bay leaves
¼ pint (150 ml) lavender flowers
¼ pint (150 ml) rosemary
½ pint (300 ml) sage leaves
1 tbsp (15 g) thyme
5 tbsp (75 g) allspice/orris mixture
3 tbsp (45 g) cinnamon/orris mixture
1 tbsp (15 g) thyme/orris mixture
1 tbsp (15 g) rosemary/orris mixture

Mix all the ingredients together in a large mixing bowl and place in a large jar or polythene bag. Seal and put away in a dark place for two to four weeks, shaking occasionally to help the mixing process.

Herb garden harvest

¼ pint (150 ml) lemon verbena leaves
½ pint (300 ml) rosemary leaves
½ pint (300 ml) lavender flowers
¼ pint (150 ml) lemon balm
1 tbsp (15 g) thyme
1 tbsp (15 g) crumbled bay leaves
¼ pint (150 ml) sage leaves
½ pint (300 ml) oregano
½ pint (300 ml) scented geranium leaves
5 tbsp (75 g) geranium/orris mixture
4 tbsp (60 g) lavender/orris mixture
1 tbsp (15 g) rose/orris mixture

Mix all the ingredients together in a large mixing bowl and place in a large jar or polythene bag. Seal and put away in a dark place for two to four weeks, shaking occasionally to help the mixing process.

Spicy lavender pot-pourri

½ pint (300 ml) lavender flowers
¼ pint (150 ml) cornflowers
¼ pint (150 ml) cloves
½ pint (300 ml) crushed cinnamon sticks
½ pint (300 ml) pink rose petals
2 tbsp (30 g) lavender/orris mixture

Mix all the ingredients together in a large mixing bowl and place in a large jar or polythene bag. Seal and put away in a dark place for two to four weeks, shaking occasionally to help the mixing process.

Moth chaser sachets

¼ pint (150 ml) Santolina, *crushed*
¼ pint (150 ml) Artemisia
¼ pint (150 ml) mint leaves
¼ pint (150 ml) rosemary leaves
5 cinnamon sticks, crushed
¼ pint (150 ml) cloves
¼ pint (150 ml) lemon peel, dried and chopped
¼ pint (150 ml) lemon-scented geranium leaves
3 tbsp (45 g) lavender/orris mixture
3 tbsp (45 g) clove/orris mixture
2 tbsp (30 g) lemon/orris mixture

Mix all the ingredients together in a large mixing bowl and place in a large jar or polythene bag. Seal and put away in a dark place for two to four weeks, shaking occasionally to help the mixing process. Use in sachets that can be hung in cupboards or laid in drawers to ward off fierce moths.

Hops have long been associated with sleep-inducing remedies. A selection of herbs may be added to a pillow or just hops alone to help promote a good night's sleep.

Christmas sachet mix

½ pint (300 ml) pine needles
½ pint (300 ml) conifer leaves
¼ pint (150 ml) bay leaves, crushed
¼ pint (150 ml) eucalyptus leaves, crushed
½ pint (300 ml) orange peel, dried and chopped
¼ pint (150 ml) cinnamon sticks, chopped
¼ pint (150 ml) allspice berries
5 tbsp (75 g) pine/orris mixture
3 tbsp (45 g) orange/orris mixture
2 tbsp (30 g) allspice/orris mixture

Mix all the ingredients together in a large mixing bowl and place in a large jar or polythene bag. Seal and put away in a dark place for two to four weeks, shaking occasionally to help the mixing process.

HOP PILLOWS

For centuries, hop pillows have been popular remedies for combating insomnia and promoting restful sleep. Originally, mattresses would have been filled with grasses and herbs, which is why the plant *Galium odorata* is commonly known as 'ladies bedstraw' or 'hedge bedstraw'. From there we progressed to stuffing pillows and mattresses with down and horsehair, but the smell of the grasses was replaced by a herbal pillow. During the Victorian era, herb pillows were much favoured, particularly ones made from lavender and roses.

Although it is traditional to slip herb pillows into the main pillowcase and therefore keep them out of sight, they look best when decorated with plenty of lace and ribbons, especially if you are giving them as a present.

Many fabrics can be used for making

pillows, ranging from plain calico that can be slipped into the main pillowcase to antique linens and lace that give a really luxurious effect and deserve to be left on show. The two most popular scents for inducing sleep are hops and lavender, but these fragrances do not blend well together so choose one or the other. Both of these recipes smell heavenly and will help you drift off into scented sleep.

Sweet hop and spice mix

2 pints (1.2 l) dried hops
2 tbsp (30 g) allspice
2 tbsp (30 g) orange peel, dried
2 tbsp (30 g) lemon balm leaves
1 tbsp (15 g) allspice/orris mixture
1 tbsp (15 g) neroli (orange blossom)/orris
* mixture*

Mix all the ingredients together in a large mixing bowl and place in a large jar or polythene bag. Seal and put away in a dark place for two to four weeks, shaking occasionally to help the mixing process.

Victorian flower sleep mix

¾ pint (450 ml) dark red or pink scented
* rose petals*
½ pint (300 ml) elderflowers
½ pint (300 ml) lavender flowers
¼ pint (150 ml) rosemary leaves (they keep
* away evil spirits!)*
5 tbsp (75 g) rose/orris mixture
3 tbsp (45 g) lavender/orris mixture

Mix all the ingredients together in a large mixing bowl and place in a large jar or polythene bag. Seal and put away in a dark place for two to four weeks, shaking occasionally to help the mixing process.

Making a hop pillow

To make a hop pillow you will need the following ingredients:

½ yard (½ metre) muslin
Sweet Hop and Spice Mix
½ yard (½ metre) plain or patterned cotton
lace or ribbons

Cut out two pieces of muslin, each approximately 14 × 12 in (35 × 30 cm), and machine or sew by hand around three sides. Turn right sides out and fill with the hop mix, then stitch up the fourth side firmly by hand. Now cut out two pieces of the cotton, slightly larger than the muslin and allowing extra for seams approximately 16 × 14 in (40 × 35 cm). Placing right sides together, machine around three sides, incorporating the lace if you wish at this stage. Turn right sides out, then turn under the seam allowance on the fourth side and place the hop pillow inside. Finish the last edge by hand with neat oversewing stitches. You can then decorate the pillow with lace or ribbons.

When the fragrance of the hop pillow begins to fade, all you have to do is remove the inner filling, replace the hop mix with a new batch and then sew up the pillow again. This is quicker and easier than having to replace loose contents in the cotton pillow.

Handkerchief pillow

The easiest way of all to make a pretty square sleep pillow is to use pretty lace-edged handkerchiefs. Most of the work is done for you then, and a pretty pillow can

be made in a very short time.

You will need:

4 lace-edged handkerchiefs
*¹/₂ yard (¹/₂ metre) plain white cotton lawn
or cotton*
¹/₂ yard (¹/₂ metre) muslin

Join the four handkerchiefs together in a square by oversewing the edges or using a zigzag stitch on a sewing machine. Cut the cotton backing to the same size as the square of four handkerchiefs and then turn in the edges by the depth of the lace so the square fits the fabric area of the four handkerchiefs. Machine-stitch around three sides of the fabric, leaving the lace free and one side open. Make a square muslin pillow as described for the hop pillow (see page 112) and fill with any of the sachet mixes (see pages 111–12) — the Victorian flowers mix might be the most suitable. Insert the muslin pad and close the pillow with small slip stitches. You can decorate the top of the cushion with some ribbon bows if you wish.

SMALL PERFUMED SACHETS

Smaller sachets have many uses: they can be tucked in drawers and cupboards, or used to scent linen cupboards or lingerie. There is nothing more glamorous than a drawer that exudes a lovely floral aroma whenever it is opened. Desks can benefit from sharper scents — if work has to go on through the night, a sachet filled with basil, to relieve tiredness, or cardamom, to help concentration, might be appropriate.

To sleep in bedlinen scented with the sweet smell of lavender has long been a luxury. Isaak Walton in 1682 recommended

a hostelry purely on those grounds.

'Good master, let's go to that house, for the linen looks white and smells of lavender, and I long to lie in a pair of sheets that smell so.'

The easiest way to make little sachets to give as presents, or to use yourself, is to buy a collection of pretty lace-edged handkerchiefs. Place a couple of table-spoons of one of the mixtures in the centre of each handkerchief, gather up the edges and tie with pretty ribbons to make an elegant and fragrant bundle.

If you wish to use a printed or plain fabric, you can cut out two pieces of fabric of the size you require, with a small allowance for seams. Sew around three sides of the main sachet and similarly on two slightly smaller pieces of muslin. Turn the muslin right sides out, fill with pot-pourri and sew up the fourth edge by hand. Turn the cotton sachet right sides out, insert the muslin sachet and sew up the fourth edge by hand. It is not essential to make the muslin liner but it does save time when renewing the sachet as you can throw away the old sachet and replace it with a new one. A liner also reduces the likelihood of the oils staining the outer cover.

PADDED COAT HANGERS WITH FRAGRANT SACHETS

Another luxury with a practical purpose is a padded coat hanger that has a matching sachet hanging from its centre. Padded hangers are much kinder to clothes than ordinary wire ones and are less likely to leave hanger marks on delicate fabrics. The sachet can be hung inside the article

of clothing, making it fresh and fragrant the next time it is worn. You can either use a flowery pot-pourri mix or the moth chaser recipe, which will keep away moths and help to protect woollen clothing in particular.

You will need:

6 wooden coat hangers
½ yard (½ metre) wadding
½ yard (½ metre) printed cotton
2 yards (2 metres) ½-in (12-mm) wide ribbon
matching cotton
extra ribbon for bows

Cut a strip of wadding 36 × 2 in (90 × 5 cm) and wind it around a coat hanger, stitching it securely at each end. To cover the hook, fold 1 in (2.5 cm) of ribbon over at one end and then bind the remaining ribbon tightly all the way down the hook. Stitch the end of the ribbon to the wadding at the base of the hook, then cut off the surplus ribbon.

Cut out a piece of the fabric about 4¾ in (12 cm) wide and slightly longer than the hanger, then fold it in half lengthwise with the right sides together. Stitch across both short ends. Turn to the right side. Neaten the raw edges on the long sides by folding the seam allowance over and pressing or tacking it into position. Press a crease line along the bottom of the casing.

Place the wadding-wrapped hanger inside the fabric casing, with the open edges along the top of the hanger. Pin in position while working. Join the seam edges with running stitch, leaving the cotton loose at the end. Also sew running stitches along the bottom crease and again leave the cotton loose at the end. Pull both ends of the hanging threads to form gathers all

along the hanger, then secure the threads tightly. The hanger can now be decorated with a large or small bow. Make a matching sachet in the same way as for the small perfumed sachets (see page 113), then hang it from the hook with some ribbon or lace.

Gentleman's mix
Most pot-pourri and sachet mixes are rather too feminine for a man's wardrobe. So, here is a mix that would suit most men and might appeal to some ladies as well!

¼ pint (150 ml) lemon verbena leaves
1 tbsp (15 g) mint leaves
1 tbsp (15 g) cloves
1 tbsp (15 g) rosemary
¼ pint (150 ml) raspberry leaves
1 tbsp (15 g) lemon/orris mixture
1 tbsp (15 g) mint/orris mixture
1 tbsp (15 g) oregano/orris mixture

Mix all the ingredients together in a large mixing bowl and place in a large jar or polythene bag. Seal and put away in a dark place for two to four weeks, shaking occasionally to help the mixing process.

A padded coat hanger is a luxury with a very practical use. Matching sachets filled with pot-pourri or a moth chaser mixture can be suspended from the hangers to complete the gift.

HERBAL POT-POURRI IN THE KITCHEN

Warmth brings out the smell of herbs, spices and all pot-pourri mixes. The first warm room in a house that you think of is the kitchen, and there are plenty of herbal gift ideas that would look lovely in a kitchen and be very practical presents too.

Herbal oven mitts

Whether the recipient is a keen cook or not, everyone uses the kitchen at one time or another and most people would be glad of a pair of attractive oven gloves. Perhaps unwilling cooks would use their ovens more if their oven gloves smelt good every time they used them.

Oven mitts can be made from a simple bought pattern or one you have made yourself by drawing a mitten shape around your hand. Add small muslin bags of chopped spices, such as the Mint and Cinnamon Mix (see page 109) or the Herb and Spice Mix (see page 109), between the heat-proof wadding and the outer cotton layer.

Herbal hot mats

The same technique can be used to make quilted herbal hot mats. Place the same mixes, in their muslin sachets, between the layers of cotton fabric and padding. This technique is also very effective for making tea cosies and egg cosies. As the spices are contained in muslin bags they can easily be removed whenever the article needs a wash.

Herbal hot water bottle covers

Another unusual gift idea would be to make or buy a hot water bottle cover and make a small pocket for it. If you place a sachet containing one of the sleep mixes, or any other mixture of your choice, in this pocket, the warmth of the hot water bottle will bring out the fragrance. When making sachets that must be very small and slim but powerful, you can fill the muslin or cotton bags with the orris root and essential oil mixture alone. This gives a very strongly scented sachet with no unnecessary bulk, and which is excellent for small nooks and crannies where a bulky sachet would be unsuitable.

Store cupboard spices

2 tbsp (30 g) powdered cinnamon
2 tbsp (30 g) powdered ginger
2 tbsp (30 g) powdered allspice
1 tbsp (15 g) cloves, crushed
2 vanilla pods, chopped
1 tsp (5 g) powdered mace
1 tbsp (15 g) powdered nutmeg
2 tbsp (30 g) dried orange peel, finely
  chopped
1 tbsp (15 g) orange/orris mixture
1 tbsp (15 g) allspice/orris mixture

Mix all the ingredients together in a large mixing bowl and place in a large jar or polythene bag. Seal and put away in a dark place for two to four weeks, shaking occasionally to help the mixing process. Use to make small sachets that you can tuck into corners of storage cupboards to give that home baking smell whenever you open the doors.

HERBAL GREETINGS CARDS

There are many ways to incorporate herbs or herbal pot-pourris into cards and communications. The language of flowers could

certainly come into its own here.

Pressed herbs lend themselves particularly to greetings cards. You could make some greetings cards decorated with a single herb and then tuck a packet of seeds for that herb inside the card. A group of herbs, perhaps the constituent parts of bouquet garni (parsley, marjoram, thyme and bay) could be used to decorate a card that accompanies a gift of bundles of bouquet garni for a keen cook. Smaller gift tags can also be made to attach to your herbal gifts. You could decorate them with little herb posies or botanical-style sprays of pressed herbs.

The pressed flowers must be glued to the front of the card with tiny dabs of latex adhesive and then covered with a clear plastic film, similar to that used to protect books (see stockists, page 126).

Dried flowers and herbs can also be displayed on greetings cards, and you can make a three-dimensional display, attaching the flowers and herbs with a strong adhesive or hot glue gun. The finished card will not fit into an envelope because it is too bulky, but it looks very professional when displayed in an acetate box.

Choosing suitable papers and cards

There are many specialist herbal papers, hand-made papers and cards that can be used as a background. Soft off-white or cream backing looks better than brilliant white, which can be too stark. Parchment is particularly effective as it gives a traditional feel to the card. Pink parchment-effect card decorated with a bunch of pink rosebuds and some herbs tied with a tiny pink ribbon would make a lovely card to welcome the arrival of a new baby girl.

Pot-pourri cards

Pot-pourri can also be incorporated into a greetings card. A small sachet can be made by cutting out two large identical flowers from a panel of lace, sewing them together and filling them with some herbal pot-pourri. This could then be attached to the front or inside of the card as a detachable sachet. There are three-fold cards available (see stockists, page 126), which enable you to have a lacy pot-pourri sachet as part of the front of the card, which you can then decorate with flowers and ribbons as in the photograph. Small garlands of herbs and flowers can encircle the cut-out section of the card, which is filled with a lacy pot-pourri sachet.

A rose design on the front of the card could be accompanied by a suitable rose quote or poem inside. A card decorated with borage could bear the recipe for a delicious Pimms No. 1 cup inside, and the card could be attached to the bottle!

SCENTED CARDS AND NOTEPAPER

All cards and paper can very easily be perfumed. A standard commercial greetings card can be perfumed by storing it in a sealed container, with a sachet of orris and essential oil mixture, for a few weeks. The same idea applies to writing paper and envelopes, which can be scented by placing a sachet of your favourite orris and oil mix in a box, laying the sheets of writing paper and envelopes over it and closing the lid. Keep the lid firmly shut for about six weeks. You could also decorate the sheets of paper with pressed flowers and cover the design with clear plastic film.

A collection of herbal bits and pieces for a keen gardener could include a selection of unusual or rare plant cuttings, Mint Pot-pourri, Minty Mustard and Mint and Tomato Chow Chow.

PACKAGING IDEAS AND GIFT COLLECTIONS FOR FAMILY AND FRIENDS

There are various ways in which herbal ideas can be collected together, without vast expense, to make unusual presents for your family and friends. Once you know they have a particular interest or enthusiasm you can base your ideas around that. I have listed some ideas here, but the best way is to think carefully about the person concerned and decide what he or she would really like. It is all too easy to spend money, but the greatest gift we can give today is our time. If you care enough about someone to make a collection of small presents, it will mean much more than casually buying an anonymous, pre-packaged gift at a large store.

A keen gardener's collection

- A collection of unusual varieties of mint, which you can either grow yourself at minimal cost or buy from a nursery or herb centre. Don't forget to label them!
- A pot of Mint and Apple Jelly (see page 68).
- A small pot of Minty Mustard (see page 69).
- A jar of Mint and Tomato Chow Chow (see page 72).
- A box of Delicious Mint and Cinnamon Pot-pourri (see page 109).

All these can be placed in a pretty basket or box, depending on your budget, and packed with straw, which is usually available from a greengrocer. Alternatively, you could use shredded tissue paper. The whole basket can then be wrapped in cellophane and tied with a green bow. The accompanying card could be decorated with some pressed mint flowers and leaves, with your message written inside.

A treasure trove for a bath addict!

We all know someone who loves spending time relaxing in the bath — don't we all! This is a special collection of unusual bath oils and perfumes that won't be given by anyone else.

- A collection of lavender, rose and neroli (orange blossom) bath bags, tied with different ribbons in shades of lilac, pink and apricot, according to the fragrance. (Make them with dried lavender flowers, rose petals or orange blossom.)
- A beautiful bottle of bath oil scented with neroli (orange blossom).
- A package of Lavender and Rose Washballs (see page 104) laid in a large sea shell that could later be used as a soap dish.
- A jar containing Orange Blossom Bath Salts (see page 104).

Arrange all these products, making sure that the bath oil has a firmly sealed top, in a basket or box. You could pad the box with toning cotton wool balls and bows. Wrap it all up in cellophane and decorate with a ribbon. The gift tag could have tiny pearl shells on the front and your message inside.

A Father's Day parcel

It is always said that it's hard to choose presents for men, but this would make a very unusual Father's Day gift, and all the family could help to make it.

- A selection of small herbal mustards (see page 69).

- A jar of Coriander Barbecue Sauce (see page 76).
- A loaf of Strawberry and Mint Soda Bread (see page 81).
- A bottle of Elderflower Champagne (see page 79).

Use an old fruit crate or orange box as a container and fill it with straw. Make sure the soda bread is well wrapped. Arrange all the goodies and add a copy of the recipient's favourite magazine. Then wrap the package in cellophane and decorate with ribbon tied in the shape of a bow tie. The gift tag could also be in the shape of a bow tie, with your message written on the reverse.

Foodie delights for a gourmet cook

There are many different items to choose from in the kitchen section of the book, but here are a few suggestions.

- A jar of Spicy Prunes with Bergamot (see page 76).
- A jar of Old-fashioned Herb Sauce (see page 78).
- A bottle of Mint and Cranberry Vinegar (see page 77).
- A bottle of Parsley and Lemon Oil (see page 77).
- A bottle of Olive Oil with Oregano (see page 78).

These goodies could all be packed into a large earthenware mixing bowl that has been padded with some traditional linen tea towels. Cover with cellophane and decorate with a gingham bow that has a wooden spoon pushed through it. The gift tag could be in the shape of a jam jar.

A package for Grandma

Older people can be rather difficult to buy presents for; they have accumulated so many things over the years that they may have very little space left! This package of luxuries will bring back happy memories of traditional recipes and give some surprises with new ones not tried before.

- A jar of Lemon and Mint Marmalade (see page 65).
- A jar of Apple and Elderflower Jam (see page 67).
- A jar of Mint and Apple Jelly (see page 68).
- A jar of Gooseberry and Lemon Balm Jelly (see page 67).

Place all these jars in a basket that will be useful once it has been emptied, either for shopping or for storing scraps of wool or fabric. Pack the basket well with straw or tissue paper and arrange the jars on top. Wrap with cellophane and decorate with a bow in the recipient's favourite colour. The gift tag could be made by one of the grandchildren — perhaps a drawing of granny or her house.

THE SECRET LANGUAGE OF FLOWERS

The language of flowers gathered momentum during the Victorian era, when what began as a symbolic use of flowers with a few obvious meanings gradually developed into a complete secret language.

Today we use many other methods of communication, which are faster and clearer, so there is no need for guesswork any more. However, there are times when it is fun to reinforce the sentiment of a gift with reference to this old and now little used language, and it is perfect for born romantics!

There are many different reference sources for this secret language, some of which are older than others. I have gathered as many flower meanings as possible and leave you to use them as you see fit!

THE SECRET LANGUAGE OF FLOWERS

Acacia, pink Elegance
Acacia, yellow Friendship
African violet Such worth is rare
Alchemilla Protection
Allspice berries Valuable, precious
Almond blossom Hope
Amaranth (globe) Unfading love
Amaryllis Pride, splendid beauty
Ambrosinia Love returned
Anemone Forsaken
Angelica Inspiration

Aniseed Indulgence
Apple blossom Preference
Aster Variety
Azalea Temperance

Bachelor's buttons Temperance
Balm of Gilead Sympathy, consolation
Basil Good wishes
Bay Glory
Begonia Dark thoughts
Belladonna Silence
Bell flower Gratitude
Bittersweet Truth
Bluebell Constancy
Borage Bluntness or courage, cheerfulness
Broom Humility

Burnet Light-hearted
Buttercup Childishness

Cactus flower Warmth
Calceolaria I offer you my fortune
Calendula Grief, cruelty in love
Camelia, red Gratitude
Camelia, white Perfected loveliness
Camomile Patience
Campanula Gratitude
Canary grass Perseverance
Candytuft Indifference
Canterbury bell Acknowledgement
Caraway Steadfast
Carnation, pink Woman's love
Carnation, red Alas for my poor heart
Carnation, striped Refusal
Carnation, yellow Disdain
Catnip Courage
Chervil Sincerity
Chestnut Do me justice
Chicory Frugality
Chrysanthemum, red I love
Chrysanthemum, white Absolute truth, fidelity
Chrysanthemum, yellow Slighted love
Cineraria Always delightful
Clematis Mental beauty, purity
Clover, four-leaved Be mine
Clover, red Industry
Clover, white Think of me
Cockscomb Singularity
Coltsfoot Maternal care
Columbine Folly
Columbine, purple Resolution
Convolvulus Uncertainty
Coreopsis Always cheerful
Coriander Hidden merit
Cowslip Pensiveness, divine beauty
Crocus Youthful, gladness
Cumin Faithfulness
Cyclamen Diffidence
Cypress Death, mourning

Daffodil Regard
Dahlia Good taste
Daisy Innocence and beauty
Dandelion Oracle
Daphne Painted lily
Dill Luck, magical charm
Dock Patience
Dogwood Durability

Eglantine, flowers Poetry
Eglantine, foliage Simplicity
Elderflower Compassion, consolation
Eucalyptus Get well, take care
Everlasting flower Unfading memory

Fennel Flattery
Fenugreek Honey sweet
Fern Sincerity, fascination
Flax Appreciation
Forget-me-not Fidelity, true love
Foxglove Insincerity
Fuchsia Taste

Gardenia Untold love
Gentian You are unjust
Geranium, scarlet Comforting friendship
Geranium, scented Preference
Geranium, ivy Bridal favour
Geranium, lemon Unexpected meeting
Geranium, nutmeg Expected meeting
Gilliflower Lasting beauty, recall
Gladioli Strong character
Globe amaranth Immortality
Gloxinia A proud spirit

Hawthorn blossom Hope
Heartsease Remembrance
Heather Admiration, protection
Heliotrope Devotion
Hibiscus Delicate beauty
Hollyhock Ambition
Honeysuckle Devoted affection, bonds of love

Horehound Health
Hyacinth, blue Games, play
Hyacinth, purple Sorrowful
Hyacinth, white Unobtrusive loveliness
Hydrangea Heartlessness
Hyssop Cleanliness, sacrifice

Iris Message
Ivy Fidelity

Jacob's ladder Come down
Jasmine, white Amiability
Jasmine, yellow Happiness, grace and
  elegance
Jonquil I desire a return of affection

Kingcups Desire for riches

Lady's slipper Capricious beauty
Lantana Rigour
Larkspur Lightness, levity or fickleness
Laurel Glory
Lavender Distrust, silence
Lemon balm Memories, longevity
Lemon blossom Fidelity in love
Lemon verbena Delicacy of feeling
Lilac, purple Love's first emotions
Lilac, white Youthful innocence
Lily, imperial Majesty
Lily, madonna Purity, sweetness
Lily, yellow Crime
Lily of the valley Return of happiness
Lobelia Malevolence
Lotus flower Mystery, truth
Love-in-a-mist Perplexity
Love lies bleeding Hopeless not
  heartless
Lupin Voraciousness

Magnolia Dignity and love of nature
Mallow Ambition, fertility
Marigold Grief, despair
Marjoram Health, happiness

Marshmallow Beneficence
Meadowsweet Uselessness
Michaelmas daisy Farewell
Mignonette Your qualities surpass your
  charms
Mimosa Sensitivity
Mint Virtue
Mock orange Counterfeit
Morning glory Affection
Mugwort Happiness or weary traveller
Myrtle Love

Narcissus Egotism
Nasturtium Patriotism
Nettle You are spiteful

Oleander Beware
Olive Peace
Orange blossom Purity, loveliness or
  bridal festivities
Orchid Rare beauty

Pansy Love, thought
Parsley Festivity
Passion flower Faith
Peach blossom I am your captive
Pennyroyal Flee away
Peony Bashfulness
Peppermint Warmth of feeling
Periwinkle, blue Early friendship
Periwinkle, white Pleasures of memory
Petunia Never despair
Phlox Our hearts are united
Pinks Love, boldness
Polyanthus Pride of riches
Poppy, red Consolation
Primrose Early youth
Primula Diffidence

Quince Temptation

Ranunculus You are radiant with charms
Rhododendron Danger, beware

Rose, cabbage Ambassador of love
Rose, china Beauty always new
Rose, damask Brilliant complexion
Rose, mundi Variety
Rose, musk Capricious beauty
Rose, red Love
Rose, red and white together Unity
Rose, white I am worthy of you
Rose, wild Simplicity
Rose, yellow Jealousy
Rosebud Pure and lovely
Rosemary Remembrance
Rue Remorse, repentance

Sage Esteem
Salvia, blue I think of you
Salvia, red Energy
Scabious Unfortunate love
Scilla, blue Forgive and forget
Snapdragon No
Snowdrop Hope
Sorrel Affection
Southernwood Constancy
Spearmint Warmth of sentiment
Speedwell Fidelity
Stephanotis You can boast too much
Stock Lasting beauty
Strawberry leaf Righteous
Sunflower Adoration
Sweet pea Lasting pleasure

Sweet William Gallantry
Syringa Memory

Tansy Hostile thoughts
Thistle Austerity
Thorn branch Severity
Thrift Sympathy
Thyme Activity
Trillium Modest beauty
Tuberose Dangerous pleasures
Tulip, red Declaration of love
Tulip, variegated Beautiful eyes
Tulip, yellow Hopeless love

Valerian Readiness
Verbena, white Pure and guileless
Veronica Fidelity
Vervain Enchantment
Violet Modesty or faithfulness

Wallflower Fidelity in adversity
Willow Mourning
Wisteria Welcome
Woodbine Fraternal love
Wormwood Absence, displeasure

Yarrow Foretelling the future
Yew Sorrow

Zinnia Thoughts of absent friends

SUPPLIERS

Dried flowers, herbs and baskets and pot pourri ingredients

Joanna Sheen Ltd
P.O. Box 52
Newton Abbot
Devon
TQ12 4YF

Tel. (0626) 872405 (Mail order and enquiries)

Joanna Sheen Ltd
7 Lucius Street
Torquay
Devon

Tel. (0803) 201311 (shop hours 9.00–5.30)

Mail order dried flowers, herbs and baskets

The Hop Shop
Castle Farm
Shoreham
Sevenoaks
Kent
TN14 7UB

Tel. (095 92) 3219

Nurseries supplying fresh herbs

Southwick Country Herbs
Southwick Farm
Nomansland
Near Tiverton
Devon

Tel. (0884) 861099
(Wholesale and retail nursery)

Suffolk Herbs
Sawyers Farm
Little Cornard
Sudbury
Suffolk
CO10 0NY

(Mail order catalogue)

General Interest

The Herb Society
77 Great Peter Steet
London
SW1 2EZ